ARISE
SIR DAVID
BECKHAM

ARISE
SIR DAVID
BECKHAM

**FOOTBALLER, CELEBRITY, LEGEND – THE BIOGRAPHY OF
BRITAIN'S BEST LOVED SPORTING ICON**

Gwen Russell

JOHN BLAKE

Published by John Blake Publishing Ltd,
3 Bramber Court, 2 Bramber Road,
London W14 9PB, England

www.johnblakepublishing.co.uk

First published in hardback in 2008
This edition published in 2011

ISBN: 978-1-84358-298-4

British Library Cataloguing-in-Publication Data:

A catalogue record for this book is available from the British Library.

Design by www.envydesign.co.uk

Printed in Great Britain by CPI William Clowes, Beccles, NR34 7TL

1 3 5 7 9 10 8 6 4 2

Papers used by John Blake Publishing are natural, recyclable products
made from wood grown in sustainable forests. The manufacturing processes
conform to the environmental regulations of the country of origin.

Every attempt has been made to contact the relevant copyright-holders,
but some were unobtainable. We would be grateful if the
appropriate people could contact us.

CONTENTS

CHAPTER 1

TO TED AND SANDRA: A SON

Ted and Sandra Beckham were ecstatic: they had just had their second child, a son. The year was 1975 and, in early May, Sandra entered Whipps Cross Hospital in Leytonstone, east London where, on the second day of that month, she gave birth to David Robert Joseph Beckham, who was to be the second of three children – Lynne, the oldest, was born a couple of years earlier and Joanna was yet to come along. And Ted, in particular, was delighted, for the arrival of a boy meant he had someone with whom to share his deepest and most abiding interest – football.

All his life, Ted had worshipped Manchester United, one of the most famous football clubs in the world, and from the start he was determined his newborn would share his passion. At first, of course, no one had any idea quite how much his son was to fulfil his dreams, for the Beckhams came from humble origins: Sandra was a hairdresser and Ted a kitchen fitter, with no idea that their son was one day going to become one of the most famous men in the world. But what they would soon know was that baby Becks would become just as fanatical about the sport as his father was.

From a very young age, David was taken by Ted to a nearby park for a kickabout and the boy soon became so keen on this new pastime that he would practise alone for hours and hours, perfecting the dead-ball kicks that are now world famous. As an adult, David once revealed that some people thought his famous free kicks were a matter of luck: they were not, he said. They were the result of unending practice stints that dated back to those very early days.

Shortly after David's birth, the family moved to Chingford, Essex, the home of his grandparents, where he was to spend the remainder of his childhood. Always an appealing little boy, David seemed to have only one drawback as far as football was concerned – his height. The young David was actually quite short – it was not until his late teens that he suddenly shot up to become the six-footer that he is now.

If David worried about his height, he didn't show it. Football became such a passion, so quickly, that it soon dominated his entire life. He would play wherever he could: not only in spaces just outside his family's houses, but also on the council pitches at Ainsley Wood School.

Away from the pitch, he was surprisingly shy. It's a quality he's retained to the present day: when he first met the then Victoria Adams, it was she who had to open the conversation.

David's first school was Chase Lane Primary School and fellow schoolmates remember his passion for his chosen sport even back then. 'We were all very quiet at school, David especially,' recalls Matthew Treglohan, who became one of David's closest friends. 'I used to sit next to him in geography and art classes. He was very good at art, but was only ever interested in football. He wasn't even that bothered about girls then. A few of the kids shone through in football, but David was certainly one of the best.'

But that is to understate the case. David was so good, so young, that his potential was spotted even before he was in his teens. It was while he was attending Chingford School that he took the first step towards what was to become his career. The local paper ran an ad reading: 'Wanted: Football stars of the future'. (Ironically, in one of the many parallels that run throughout their lives, Victoria also kicked off her career when she spotted an ad for singers and dancers in a paper, although in her case she was in her late teens.) David got in touch and soon began playing for the Ridgeway Rovers in the Enfield Sunday League. The team, David's local outfit, played in what is now called the Peter May Sports Ground in Wadham Road, Highams Park. It is fair to say he made his mark: in the course of three years, he scored over 100 goals, while also playing for another team, Chingford High, in the Waltham Forest District and Essex Under-15s.

3

A fellow school footballer, Nana Boachie, remembers it well. 'We were both 11 in our first proper football contest and David desperately wanted to start off with a goal,' Nana says. 'As goalie on the opposing side, I wanted to keep a clean sheet. He just said, "We'll see," in that quiet voice of his. Just before half-time, we gave away a free kick just outside the area. David curled the ball into the top corner. It was impossible to save. He still remembers it.'

So proficient did the young David show himself to be that top clubs began to notice him. He might have been only 11, but London clubs Tottenham Hotspur and Arsenal both began making enquiries about this extraordinarily talented young man. But, despite the fact that he lived just outside London, David wasn't interested. He knew who he wanted to play for and it wasn't a London club at all – it was Manchester United. Ted Beckham was a stalwart fan of United and now his son was, too. He got teased about it, as well.

'I used to take so much stick from my mates at school,' David confessed. 'I had a couple of mates who were West Ham fans and a couple who were Tottenham or Arsenal fans. But I remember when we beat Arsenal 6–2, Sharpey [Lee Sharpe] scored the hat-trick. I used to wear my United shirt over my school uniform on my way to school, so I got a lot of stick, but I used to give a lot back.'

It is noticeable, incidentally, that even then David was going to wear what he wanted, regardless of what anyone else thought. Indeed, David was to become interested in clothes

4

very early on. But, to fund that habit and much else besides, he had to earn some money and so got a job as a potman at Walthamstow Dog Stadium, where he earned the princely sum of £10 a night. And it was at this young age that David got a taste of what was to come. In 1986, he took part in the TSB Bobby Charlton Soccer Skills final, which he won – the youngest competitor ever to have done so. And that final took place at Old Trafford, Manchester United's home ground, which meant that David first kicked a ball there when he was only 11. Funnily enough, the prize was also a little taste of what was to come: it was a two-week trip to Spain to train with Barcelona. Terry Venables was the manager and players included Mark Hughes, Steve Archibald and Gary Lineker.

Nor was that the only foretaste of what his later life was to be like. The competition at Old Trafford took place on the same day as a match with Tottenham Hotspur, and so there were plenty of Spurs fans present. Despite David's tender years, the fans were not shy about making clear what they thought of his choice of team. 'All the Spurs fans were there and, as I was doing the dribbling in and out of the cones, they noticed that this was David Beckham of Essex,' he said. 'The Spurs fans started singing and cheering, but then the announcer said I was a Man United fan. They booed me and I went in to a couple of cones.'

It was fortunate that David was showing such promise on the pitch, because he certainly wasn't shining at school. Blessed with only limited academic ability, he clearly spent most of his time in lessons wishing he could get out of them, as evidenced by a number of tersely worded school reports dating from when he was 12. 'David is continually silly, which he cannot afford to be if he wishes to make progress,' his French teacher wrote. 'I can only hope for a more mature approach.'

The French teacher was not alone: none of the others seemed to rate David's abilities very highly, either. 'His behaviour has been extremely silly,' thundered the doyenne of Home Economics. 'Could do a lot better.'

'David has ability but finds it difficult to concentrate,' wrote his Humanities teacher. 'His attitude must improve immediately if he is to fulfil his potential.'

Indeed, it would appear that the only field he was excelling in was the playing field – but even here he came in for criticism. 'David has a natural ability to succeed at most sports,' said his sports teacher, in a reflection that was to prove emphatically correct. 'But he should be careful of distractions, which affect his application.'

As for David himself? 'I would have enjoyed lessons at school more if we'd talked about football,' he said. 'But I was quite good at art – maybe I'd have gone into that if I had not got my break in soccer.'

If truth be told, David was never destined for academia. His greatest enjoyment when confined to the classroom was causing disruption, not swotting for his exams, and his friends felt the same way, too. 'To be honest, teachers used to find David and his friends hard to control,' said a teacher who had once taught at the school. 'He and six or seven of his cronies were together in the same class. They caused quite a few problems. The girls were very bright, very hardworking. But the boys wouldn't listen or pay attention. There'd be paper flicking or jostling around. David would be in the middle of that somewhere. They were boys straight out of a comic at times.'

Outside of school, however, the older generation was taking a very different attitude to the young Beckham. Winning the competition at Old Trafford and his subsequent spell in Barcelona had made him keener than ever on all things football, and the clubs continued to circle. Tottenham Hotspur was still keen and enticed David to spend some time with its school of excellence. Leyton Orient also offered him a trial. And, finally, the great Manchester United joined in: their talent scout, Malcolm Fidgeon, had heard talk of a remarkably talented young footballer resident in Essex and so attended a match in which David was playing for the Waltham Forest Under-12s against Redbridge. David's mother found out about Fidgeon's presence and alerted her son that a very big opportunity indeed might have presented itself.

'I leaped into the air and started to cry,' said David. 'It was a dream come true. It was one of my best games for the district. Being from London and being a southerner, I never thought I would get seen by a scout of Man United. But then I was lucky enough one day and I had a good game for my district side. I remember getting changed and I walked out and my mum called me over – my dad was working. There was excitement in her voice when she said, "It's lucky you had a good game, because there was a scout here from Man United and he wants to talk to Dad to discuss taking you to the club for trials."'

It was a dream come true, not only for David, but for his father, too. Ted Beckham's loyalty to Manchester United had never wavered and the fact that there was a chance that his son was to play with the team he supported was as exciting an event as anything that had happened in his life up until now. David was pretty excited too and, when he was just 14, he signed up as a schoolboy associate of United. The club itself, of course, did not yet realise quite what a treasure they had in their hands, but hopes were high right from the start.

'David is a good prospect,' said a United spokesman. 'We are delighted that he is joining us.'

It was one of those rare moments in life where just about everyone involved had got what they wanted.

Until then, David's most important footballing mentor had been his father, but now he was to meet the man who transformed him from amateur to professional: Eric Harrison. Harrison was the youth coach at United and as such was to take charge of the young Beckham's progress. Indeed, Harrison's input to David's career should not be underestimated: it was he, quite as much as Sir Alex Ferguson, who turned David into the player he is today.

Harrison was modest about his abilities. 'A good football coach is like a good school teacher – they realise the youngsters are the important ones,' he said. 'We do it for the kids, not for our own egos. I have taken so much pleasure from seeing young players develop both as footballers and people. David Beckham might have funny haircuts and lead a different life from the rest of us, but the important thing is, he's a really good kid, as well. Respect was a word I used all the time to Beckham, Giggs and the other players at United. We as adult coaches respect the youngsters and in return the youngsters should also be respectful. I am a hard taskmaster and never let the kids at United step out of line or become arrogant. Players should be confident, yes, but not arrogant where they think they know it all.'

David took these lessons and a good deal more to heart. Something else that he has in common with Victoria is that both were absolutely focused on what they wanted to do in their careers from a very early age and, to this end, David was different from his peer group. While they went out and partied, he stayed home and trained. 'I gave up a lot when I was younger, going out with the lads, parties and discos, leaving my family,' he said. 'It wasn't easy, but I knew it was what I wanted to do. I used to tell everyone and they'd laugh and say, "Yeah, but what else you gonna do?" I'd say, "No, football." United was the dream.'

Football was not the only sport in which David was competing and winning. Four years in a row he won the Essex 1500-metre championship, impressing everyone with his stamina and determination. Other clubs continued to try to tempt him away from his beloved United, but he wasn't having any of it. Wimbledon was one: manager Joe Kinnear tried hard to get him to Selhurst Park, Wimbledon's playing field, but with no luck. 'Beckham must have been about 15,' said Kinnear. 'He was a quiet lad but obviously mad on football and I wanted him. But he told me he had his heart set on going to Old Trafford.'

Indeed, he had and he finally did so in 1991, at the age of 16. It was a tender age to be leaving home, especially for a shy young man like David, but he was to realise a lifelong dream: the beginning of his career at Old Trafford. Not that anyone realised quite how auspicious a career it was going to be, though there were hints, according to Annie Kay who, with her husband Tommie, gave David digs when he first went to Manchester. Firm United supporters and now in their seventies, the Kays had been providing lodgings for young Manchester United players for 30 years.

'When David first came down, I never thought this could be the future England captain,' Annie Kay recalled. 'Having said that, he was always dedicated and a very smart dresser. When he came with his clothes, he had brought seven bags – most young footballers just had two. I said, "You've got some bags!" He said, "I've got some more!" He was very clothes conscious even when he was 16 and stood out in the neighbourhood. The girls loved him, but he wasn't bothered. He'd always be very friendly and always talk but he was very keen on his football. There was not much time for girlfriends.'

It is usually Victoria who is credited for turning David into the male fashion icon he is today, but, according to Annie, David may well have managed it without her. 'Victoria has improved him a bit, but he was very fashion-conscious before he ever met her,' Annie recalls. 'He was never a slob. He was always picky and he'd sort his own room out; he said, "Give me my bedding and I'll change my bed." There wasn't a thing out of place in his room. Not like some of the others we've had here. I'd give Mark Hughes his shirts and everything and he'd drop them on the floor. I'd pick him up but he'd say, "I know where everything is if it's on the floor."'

The Kays' house was convenient for training: it was right next to The Cliff, in Salford, which is where United used to train at the time. And the digs were a find. David had actually stayed in two other places before coming upon the Kays, both of which he'd had to leave – the first because one of his fellow players behaved badly and David got caught up in the row, and the second because he didn't like the food, which didn't go down well with his landlady. But, with the Kays, he found a real home from home, one which was to nurture him while his real family was back in the south.

Beckham himself is well aware of how lucky he was. 'My third home in Manchester is the one that holds the greatest affection,' he wrote in *David Beckham: My World*, the first of his autobiographies. 'It was the home in Lower Broughton of the terrific Annie and Tommie Kay. Mark Hughes, a legend in my eyes, stayed in the room that I had for a number of years.'

11

Indeed, the Mark Hughes connection was what had initially attracted him to the Kays. 'This was the one place he wanted to come to because Mark Hughes was here and he was his hero,' Annie recalled. 'What a prospect! I didn't know he had the talent then, but he was something special. He lived and breathed football and never got injured.'

It was also the perfect place for a young footballer to grow up. 'It was just like being an addition to their own family – and the great thing, especially for a teenager, was that they allowed me to have my own space,' David wrote.

Not that David was exactly a tearaway. He hadn't got this far to throw away the stunning opportunities now afforded to him and was training just as hard as ever without going wild on the side. Indeed, the only indulgences he allowed himself were, inevitably, fashion and shopping out of his £29.50 weekly wage – something his teammates were quick to pick up.

'He's always been a flash Cockney,' said Ryan Giggs, one of David's fellow players. 'Even at 17 when we all had Honda Preludes, he had a leather interior and a personalised licence plate.'

Another teammate was Gary Neville. 'I still remember coming across him in the youth teams,' he recalled. 'All of us local lads, such as Nicky Butt, me and Paul Scholes, wondered who this flash Cockney was. He always used to have the latest United tracksuit and the club clearly rated him.'

Nor was David the only exceptional talent coming on board. David and his teammates came variously to be known as

Fergie's Fledglings or The Class of 1992, simply because of the mass of new talent now at the club: others included the Neville brothers, Nicky Butt, Ryan Giggs (who featured in a poster Victoria stuck up on her wall in the very earliest days of the Spice Girls) and Paul Scholes.

Whatever might have happened since, it was a coup on the part of Alex Ferguson. Indeed, he allowed himself to be quietly pleased about the quality of the players he had brought on board, and, in an interview shortly after Keith Gillespie hit the headlines after a stunning match against Bury and a few months after United won the FA Youth Cup, he said as much.

'There are more like Keith in our youth team and we are looking closely at them,' he confided. 'We don't like to go overboard about young players, but this lot are very exciting. With their ability and desire to play, they should go far. Winning the FA Youth Cup can be significant. When United last won it in 1964, it triggered the best period in the club's post-Munich period. We have 18 trainees and every one of them will be given a full professional contract at 18. We don't have any doubt about them making their mark in the game. To have them all come through like this is very rare. Now it's just a matter of fitting them into the first team when the occasion arises.'

Even so, although David was clearly a very gifted player, it took some time before he was allowed to prove himself on the pitch. During his first year, when he wasn't training, he and his fellow trainees were expected to do menial tasks such as cleaning the older footballers' boots. And it took a whole year

13

before he was finally allowed out on the field: in 1992 he was brought on as a substitute for Andrei Kanchelskis in the League Cup tie against Brighton. The game ended 1–1 and four months later David made another step closer to his ultimate dream when he signed his professional contract.

Alex Ferguson wasn't the only one to be aware of the quality of his players. Bobby Charlton, who had been the David Beckham of his day and who was now a director of United, was equally impressed by all the talent now in the team. 'People say Alex should be handed the Old Trafford manager's job for life if he brings us the title this season for the first time in 26 years,' he said. 'But he already has the job for as long as he wants it. He deserves it for all the work he has put in at Old Trafford in the last six years and not just with the first team.

'What really impresses me about Manchester United under Alex's management is not the way the first team are playing – it's the future that fills me with such confidence. Of course, we fancy our chances of taking the title this season. It's going to be either us, Aston Villa or Blackburn. But I fancy our chances just as strongly in the FA Youth Cup, which we won last season. We are already in the fourth round against Wimbledon and I'm certain we'll go all the way again. That's how highly I rate the kids Alex has brought into the club.

'I've never known us – or any club in England – to have so many potentially brilliant youngsters. We have so many we are actually having to turn some very talented teenagers away. When I see these kids, I get really excited. They are an absolute joy, the way they play. Five or six of this year's youth team are certain to fix in the Premier League in the next couple of seasons. They are already that good. And it's all down to Alex Ferguson.'

With such an array of dazzling talent to compete with, perhaps it's not surprising that David was still not outshining the rest. If anything, he wasn't coming along as fast as some of his peers, which was one reason that Sir Alex decided to loan him for a month in early 1995 to Preston. It was to prove to be the making of him, although David certainly didn't think so at the time.

'I definitely didn't want to go – that's nothing against Preston,' he said. 'I was gutted really because I felt my career was over at Manchester United. The manager assured me it wasn't and it's the best thing I've ever done in my career, going to Preston. I scored straight from a corner on my debut and from a free kick in my second game, so things went quite well.'

What David really needed was to be toughened up, and the spell at Preston did exactly that. Gary Neville, who was fast becoming David's best friend, said as much. 'He thought that was the end of him at United,' he said. 'We all knew he had great ability but people said he was a bit soft going into tackles and headers. Going into the Third Division with Preston and having people kick lumps out of him toughened him up.'

And not only did it toughen him up: it showed him that there were distinct advantages in playing for Manchester United. 'Usually, you walk into United and your kit's laid out, nice brand-new towel, nice clean everything – underwear, shorts, the lot,' he later recalled. 'I turned up there and there was nothing. They had to give me odds and sods from all over the place.' And worse was to come – he had to wash his own kit.

And it was while he was with Preston that the David Beckham of today first really began to emerge. Although he was only there for a month, he scored twice, and one of those scores was the first time anyone had seen one of his trademark free kicks. He made appearances in the league five times.

After that, Ferguson felt David and the rest of the youngsters were finally ready to make their mark, and so set about getting them on to the team. The only problem about doing so was that there was no room for them, and so, to make room, Kanchelskis, Paul Ince and Mark Hughes were sold off.

David was utterly overwhelmed. 'When I was coming through the ranks, I didn't see any light at the end of the tunnel for me because there was Andrei who was flying,' he said. 'Then, all of a sudden, the door opened when the manager sold them and got us youngsters in.'

History was to prove that Sir Alex had made exactly the right move, but at the time many commentators were appalled. Among them was Alan Hansen, himself a former footballer and now a commentator on BBC's *Match of the Day*, who made his disquiet known, saying, 'You can't win anything with kids.'

Sir Alex – and Bobby Charlton – knew otherwise.

It was the start of an exhilarating time for Beckham. In

April 1995, he left Preston to return to the team and soon after made his Premier League debut in a match against Leeds United. His form improved steadily and then, to the great joy of everyone involved, he managed to score the winning goal against Chelsea in the FA Cup semi-final. Ted was as jubilant as his son: it was a dream come true for both of them.

And the fact that there was so much talent out there on the Manchester United pitch merely served to push the players further. Each wanted to be the best and the fact that the competition was so intense made them compete even harder. David trained hard, played hard and kept to the straight and narrow and, in August 1996, he was finally rewarded with the goal that made his name. Ironically, it was at Selhurst Park against Wimbledon, the very club that had tried to get David on board some years earlier when he was still barely more than a child. The goal in question was a beauty scored from the halfway line to beat Neil Sullivan, who was out in front of his area.

'It changed my life,' said David. 'The ball seemed to be in the air for hours and it all went quiet. Then the ball went in and it just erupted. I was on cloud nine. I just wanted to shake everyone's hand and stay out on the pitch for half an hour.'

That goal did quite a number of things. It strengthened the bond between Sir Alex and his young protégé – for it was at around this time that Ferguson almost seemed to be a second father to David. He was proud of the young Beckham for his dedication and talent, and anxious to encourage him to ascend the very heights of the game. It also attracted the attention of another man, one who was to play an extremely influential role in David's future career. That man was the then England manager Glenn Hoddle, who was incredibly impressed by what he saw out there on the field that day. A month later, David played in the England team against Moldova for the first time.

It is difficult to overstate quite how well David was doing at this juncture. By the end of the 1996/7 season, he had played in all the World Cup-qualifying games; he had been voted the PFA Young Player of the Year; he had reached the European Cup semi-finals; and his beloved Manchester United had won both the Premiership and the FA Cup in 1996. He was quite clearly a major star in the making.

But, for all that, David was still well known only among the footballing community. He had a certain flashiness about him, certainly, as testified to by the likes of Ryan Giggs and Gary Neville, but there was no indication of what was to come. There was no jewellery back in those days apart from the odd glitzy watch and there was certainly no nail polish or talk of facials. David was still a straightforward young man with a brilliant career to look forward to, and on top of that there was no conflict at all between him and Sir Alex Ferguson. They both wanted David to be the best and he was doing everything in his power to get there. But the time was fast approaching when there was going to be a change in all of this. David was not far off from the most significant meeting of his life. Indeed, in the theatre that was now his life, it would be fair to say there was a pop star waiting in the wings.

CHAPTER 2

V IS FOR VICTORIA...

David might have been succeeding beyond all expectation at his chosen career, but to his very great credit he was managing to retain a sense of proportion. David has always had a certain innate modesty and this was clearly manifesting itself as he began to adjust to the knowledge that he was becoming a star.

'You cannot afford to let things go to your head,' he said. 'First of all you'd get hammered by the other lads, then you have to face up to the boss. The first sign that you're getting carried away and he comes down on you like a ton of bricks. I know how difficult it's been just breaking into the first team and I'm not going to do anything to put that at risk. On the pitch sometimes it's beyond your control but it's down to you and I would be stupid to think I'm something special.'

Sir Alex was clearly a key figure in keeping the boys' feet on the ground, but David was also aware that he was following in the footsteps of some very illustrious predecessors.

'Anyway, how can someone as inexperienced as me try to be big-time when I look at the players alongside me?' he continued. 'They've probably forgotten more than I'll ever know. People like Peter Schmeichel, Eric Cantona and Gary Pallister have won just about everything going – and all I've done is scratch the surface. Hopefully, in a few years I will be able to sit back and think I've achieved something, but at the moment I'm just struggling to hold down a first-team place.'

His attitude was all the more remarkable given what the people around him were saying. It was becoming quite clear that David was turning into a world-class player and others in the field had no doubts about what a coming star they had on their hands.

'Different class,' said Graham Rix, who was working with Glenn Hoddle to train the young players. 'You can look at players of that age and tell the ones who will fail and who will make it, and those who will be stars. Becks is going to be a true star. Everybody knows what he can do with a ball at his feet, but that's not as important as what goes on away from game situations. Tell him something in training and it's done instantly; ask him to do something and there's no moans, raised eyebrows or questions, he just does it.

'A manager or coach is always looking for somebody who can take what they demand on to the pitch and impart it to other players. Tony Adams is the perfect example – a manager in player's kit – and I think that this is what Becks will develop into. He's still learning his trade, but give him five years and I think Alex Ferguson will regard him as his general.'

As it happens, David was never to achieve his ultimate dream, that of captaining United, although captaining England would certainly go some way to being a consolation. But he was well aware from the start quite how important it was to have a good captain, as he said when the former United captain Steve Bruce left to go to Liverpool.

'To have someone like Steve in the dressing room was a blessing for all the youngsters,' said David. 'He was a father figure, the person we could all turn to if there was something wrong. I was very close to him. He'd helped sort out a few problems I'd had and, with his advice, I think I came out stronger, a better person as well as player. Now he's not here, we will have to learn to stand on our own feet. There are other players you can talk to, obviously, but Brucie was a bit special when it came to giving the kids a boost. It's strange not having him around.'

Indeed, at this stage in his career, David was still very much deferring to the older and more established players. He didn't yet have the confidence he gained when he linked up with Victoria and gave the impression of being very much in awe of the company in which he found himself. He practically hero-worshipped Eric Cantona.

'You can't put into words what Eric means to us,' he said. 'Just having him on the pitch wearing a red shirt is more of a boost than you could ever explain. Other teams are frightened of him, I'm convinced of that. They know how dangerous he can be and that is worth a goal start to us. He's also been brilliant with the young players. He doesn't say too much, stand up at the blackboard and give us coaching lessons or anything, but a simple word of advice now and again often means more than a thousand coaching sessions. You only play with people like that once in your career. My hero was Bryan Robson. I wasn't around when he was at his best, but I'm just as proud to say I played in the same team as Eric Cantona.'

Of course, David did have a life outside of football, although until then it had very much taken second place to his career. One early girlfriend was Leoni Marzell, who, like David, came from Essex and she made a very telling comment about where her boyfriend's interests lay. 'He'd rather talk about Arsenal all night with my dad than enjoy a bedroom romp with me,' she remarked.

David also had relationships with Anna Bartley and Julie Killilea, but neither was particularly serious – he was merely a young man having fun. But the position of women in his life was about to make a radical change in 1997, when he first met the artist then known as Posh Spice.

It is now often forgotten that, when David and Victoria first met, she was the massively famous superstar and he was the young ingénue. The Spice Girls, one of the most successful and bestselling girl groups ever, had launched themselves the previous year and, while no one seemed to be quite sure who they were or where they had come from, everyone seemed keen to buy their records. Behind the scenes and away from the chat about Girl Power and snogging boys, the show was being run with military efficiency by the girls' manager, Simon Fuller, and their record label, Virgin, but, fronting the show, the girls were having a whale of a time.

It is quite clear in retrospect that none of them realised quite how lucky they'd been – who would, in that position? – and Victoria's early fame was eventually more than counterbalanced in the eyes of most people when David became an international celebrity. At the time, when a Spice Girl met a footballer, theirs seemed to be the perfect match in a celebrity-obsessed age.

Like David, Victoria's background was in Essex. The then Victoria Adams was born on 17 April 1974 in Harlow, Essex, before the family moved to Goff's Oak in Hertfordshire. Her parents, Tony and Jackie, built up a successful electrical wholesaling business which was how Posh got her nickname: her father was rich enough to drive a Rolls-Royce. And it must be said, the match seemed fated to be. Both David and Victoria were attracted to one another before they actually met: in David's case, after seeing her prancing around in a black catsuit in the video for the Spice Girls' second single 'Say You'll Be There' and, in Victoria's, after a magazine asked her to pick the most attractive from a group of photographs of footballers. She chose David.

The actual meeting first took place in March 1997. Victoria

wasn't interested in football, but her fellow Spice Girl Mel C was and she decided to attend a match at Old Trafford with Simon Fuller. Knowing David would be playing, Victoria decided to accompany them. David's first clue that there was someone he might want to meet in the crowd came when said crowd started booing – because Mel C supported Liverpool. After asking what was going on, David, to his utter delight, was informed that two of the Spice Girls were present.

'I jumped up and said, "Which ones? Which ones?"' said David. 'But whoever said it couldn't remember. And it was a struggle to get my mind back on the match.'

Even though he was desperate to meet her, David very nearly blew his chances in the players' bar afterwards. Victoria and Mel were holding court: paralysed with shyness, David didn't have the courage to approach the object of his desire. It was left to Victoria to make the first move, which she did with aplomb, strolling up to him and asking, 'Good game?'

And so show-business history was made.

'I do believe in love at first sight and from our first meeting I knew he was the man I wanted to spend the rest of my life with,' Victoria said.

One witness to the momentous events was Steve Aspey, a bystander in the bar. Realising he was viewing the opening scenes unfold of one of the most public romances ever, he could certainly see the two were getting on well. 'It really was a case of: "Their eyes met across a crowded room",' he said. 'Proper love at first sight. Posh spotted Becks looking at her and made a beeline straight for him. After that, they were totally wrapped up in each other. It was lovely. You could tell Becks was extremely nervous in the crowded Old Trafford players' bar. She and Mel C were getting loads of attention. But all the time Victoria was looking around as if she wanted to see someone in particular. With hindsight, she was on the look-out for Becks. He arrived and got a pint of orange juice. Posh was drinking red wine and marched straight over to him.

'I asked them both if they would mind having their photo taken with my 14-year-old lad Paul. They were super to him and agreed straight away. But it was obvious that they just wanted to be left alone. The packed room could have been completely deserted as far as they were concerned. They just kept looking into each other's eyes. Posh was a bit chubbier than she is these days. She even had a bit of a double chin. But she still looked fantastic in an unbuttoned shirt that showed her bra. I could see Becks eyeing her up and down as she did most of the talking. Then they swapped phone numbers – their love affair had started.'

Now that they had actually made contact, David was determined not to let the moment pass. He wanted a relationship with Victoria and he wanted it straight away. 'Well, I was wondering, Victoria, if you weren't doing anything after the game, I mean, perhaps we could have dinner?' he asked.

Victoria, however, was on a very tight leash in those days and had to move on with Mel C and Fuller. Becks promised he'd call. 'You'd better,' said Posh.

At first the relationship was kept secret, because everyone involved realised that the story, when it broke, would be enormous. That, incidentally, was entirely because of Victoria's celebrity. But, back then, when David was just another up-and-coming footballer, Posh's privacy had to be protected and, so, for their first date, the two ended up in Mel C's flat.

Right from the start there have been separations in the relationship and, indeed, before they got the chance to go out again, Victoria had to go to New York with the Spice Girls. But there is another feature of the relationship that stems back to its earliest days: the use of the mobile phone, and so they were able to keep in touch before they met up again.

Victoria had already disposed of one small inconvenience, her boyfriend Stuart Bilton, and so now the two were determined to spend as much time together as was humanly possible. Even so, David was backward about coming forward.

'For the first three dates he was so shy he didn't kiss me,' said Victoria. 'He finally got round to it while we were at my parents' house after our fourth date. It was worth the wait.'

And there was yet another constant throughout the relationship already in place – Victoria's parents. Victoria's is an extremely close-knit family and, right from the very start, it was a case of David fitting into the Adams family, rather than Victoria, despite her surname, becoming a Beckham. Over the longer term, alas, it was to cause problems, when Beckham was hired in Spain and Victoria's mother Jackie encouraged her daughter to stay in England – not, perhaps, the best advice to a woman married to a young, handsome, virile and massively sought-after man.

Back in 1997, news of the relationship slowly began to seep out, as it was inevitable that it would. They were seen in a nightclub together, after which it became known that Victoria had introduced David to her parents. 'Everything in her life is wonderful at the moment,' said Jackie. 'She's on top of the world. We've been told not to talk about David.'

Indeed, one person who was keen to keep matters private for as long as possible was the Spice Girls' manager Simon Fuller. Initially, he had been keen on the publicity the relationship would create, but he foresaw, well before anyone else, that the publicity would become too much. To a public massively disillusioned by the collapse of that other fairytale relationship, Prince Charles and Princess Diana, there was a palpable need to believe that some famous couple, somewhere, could be happy. And, indeed, David and Victoria's relationship did cater to that need for years until, as Fuller foresaw, the publicity surrounding their marriage fell in on itself and threatened to destroy what was undeniably one of the strongest marriages on Planet Celebrity.

As the relationship prospered, the couple became increasingly open about their feelings for one another, and the fact that they were both celebrities helped. 'I fancied David long before we met,' said Victoria. 'I wasn't attracted by his fame but, as we got to know each other, we realised it was a great bonus. We are equally famous and attract equal attention.

27

We're in the same boat and that brought us together very quickly. We used to go out in disguises – hats, glasses, all sorts of ridiculous clothes.'

On the subject of clothes, it was also at this time that David began to be a little more experimental with his look. Victoria's influence had already begun.

It was obvious almost from day one that this was it for both of them. The all-important Adams clan approved: 'David is a wonderful young man and he treats Victoria very well,' said Jackie. 'They see quite a lot of each other, despite the fact that they both have very hectic lives. Of course, David would be welcomed into our family. He is such a decent guy. I couldn't ask for more for my daughter. There's been a lot of speculation about Victoria and David but the future really is up to them.'

Like Victoria, David felt that their joint celebrity was a help rather than a hindrance to the relationship.

'That's normal,' he said of the publicity the two were attracting. 'I'm a footballer and she's a Spice Girl. It would be silly if we did not think the media and public were attracted to us. But we are just two normal young people going out together. It helps that Victoria is famous. It helps with the pressure if she is involved, because we both share it. We do understand the pressure, even though we are only 22 and 23. We are learning together. I don't see myself as front-page news but going out with Victoria I am going to get it. It is something we must handle.'

And handle it they did – rather well, in fact. As David's

profile soared – Victoria's was already stratospheric – the lucrative sponsorship deals that have contributed so strongly to the couple's wealth began to pour in. The first was a sponsorship deal with Brylcreem, for which David was paid £1 million. He was earning rather more on the pitch than he had been as a trainee, too, given that he was now being paid £10,000 a week. There were clear signs that he was beginning to enjoy the finer things in life: a Cartier was the start of a serious watch collection, while high-street labels were being replaced by the designer variety.

David was a tiny bit concerned at the effect all of this might have on his image, but, if truth be told, he could handle that, too. 'I know that dating Victoria has doubled the interest in me. We like to go for quiet meals together, but we always seem to be photographed shopping. I sometimes think people must think I live in Gucci and Prada shops. I worry that fans will forget I play football as well as go out with a Spice Girl. But I've turned down a lot of sponsorship offers because I want to be known as a footballer.'

One person who had most certainly not forgotten that David was a footballer and who was far from pleased about recent developments was Sir Alex Ferguson. His relationship with David up until now really had been as a surrogate father, but, as the fuss surrounding Posh and Becks intensified, Sir Alex became increasingly concerned about the effect it would have on David's football. In a very short space of time, David had gone from being a footballer known mainly in sporting circles to one half of the most high-profile couple in the world and Ferguson didn't like it one bit. He wanted his boys to train hard, take proper rest and have a bit of fun at the weekends. What was happening to David was something else all together. And so, like the bad fairy at the feast, he made his displeasure known – in this case, of course, on the football pitch.

The very first indication that all was not well between Beckham and his mentor came in August 1997, just five months after David and Victoria first met. Sir Alex had become increasingly irritable about the amount of time David spent on his mobile to his new girlfriend, but until now that irritation was kept on the training pitch. Now it spilled out in public when Ferguson dropped David from a match against Chelsea at Wembley and sent him to play in a friendly against Bournemouth instead.

The rest of the world had hitherto been unaware of the problems fermenting in the dressing rooms of Old Trafford and reacted with a mixture of shock and dismay.

'David is a world-class player and this is an insult to him,' said Tommy Docherty, who had himself been a manager at Manchester United. 'I think the young man has handled himself superbly. Ferguson says that you take a long-term view on players. It's lucky that Brazil didn't take a long-term view on Pele. Beckham has been an absolute model pro. He's a good lad and this decision doesn't make sense.'

But it did in Ferguson's eyes. In his view, David was putting his girlfriend before his football and so he should be punished on the football pitch. Not that he put it like that publicly, of course. Instead he merely commented, 'I was concerned about the tournament at the end of the last season in France. There is a price to pay for it. Gary Neville admitted to me that he felt really tired before he even went there.

'As far as David is concerned, we are fortunate in having a tremendous midfield of Paul Scholes, Nicky Butt and Roy Keane. I can add David when I feel the time is right, in two or three weeks. I believe we're doing the right thing for him. He is still immature as a player. He has still got a frame to fill – he will add a few more pounds. He is a later developer than some of the other young players. We will keep an eye on him.'

And so there was yet another constant in the relationship between David and Victoria – the disapproval of Sir Alex Ferguson was in there right from the start.

The relationship between David and Victoria strengthened almost by the hour, with Victoria's influence becoming ever more obvious. At her instigation, David bought a £70,000 Porsche, and, schedule permitting, she became a regular at the home he now had in Cheshire. United fans, meanwhile, seemed to share Sir Alex's view of the situation and would loudly taunt David when he went out on the pitch.

'Top players will always get that kind of stick, but they grow up at Manchester United knowing it's the price they may have to pay for playing here,' he said. 'The entire team get stick, but some players take more than others and now David is under the spotlight. He is getting quite a bit of abuse, but he just has to handle it like Ryan Giggs has and like Mark Hughes and Eric Cantona did when they were here.'

The message was clear: like it or lump it – and what do you expect if you go out with a Spice Girl?

But nothing and no one was going to come between David and his new girlfriend. If you are in the fortunate position of having met your soul mate and in the even more fortunate position of realising you have, then you are going to hang on to that person, no matter what anyone else might say. And the couple's profile continued to soar. This was the time when the Spice Girls were at the height of their fame which would have been enough to ensure saturation media coverage of their private lives, but, more than that, David and Victoria were becoming something else. Together, they were quite clearly more than the sum of their parts.

Even so, David remained as conscientious a player as he had always been and he was becoming more successful than ever on the pitch. 'That [the 1996/7 season] was the best of my career, so I've sat down with my dad and the manager to talk about how to keep it at that level,' David said. 'We all feel I can still get better. Alex Ferguson told me to rest a lot, practise a lot, look after myself and, most importantly, just concentrate on my football and nothing else.'

Credit where credit's due – Sir Alex clearly wasn't giving up the fight.

As the relationship grew stronger still, David was increasingly candid about how he and Victoria managed to cope. 'Victoria is used to the fame and all the adulation,' he said. 'We talk about it a lot. It helps. Football has become like show business, which is something in the game everybody will have to contend with. When you're a kid, all you want is to play football – you don't anticipate everything that comes with it, like the sponsorship deals and all the fame and people noticing you when you're out. You have to understand how people are and what you are to them. I am still coming to terms with it but I will be able to cope.'

And, of course, Victoria was helping him to do just that. Both were adamant that what they really wanted was a normal relationship: the fact that they were now more famous than just about anyone else in the world didn't change that.

'We take every opportunity to enjoy our privacy,' said David. 'We'd like a little more. But we know we are high-profile people. It would be the same for me whatever I did because of Victoria's business. We would like to lead normal lives and do things that don't get noticed. But I have put myself in that situation because of what I am doing on the field. Now it is a case of dealing with what happens off it.'

Victoria took a similar line. 'We buy each other presents and I love to buy my friends and family gifts because I can,' she said. 'I'm lucky that money isn't a worry now. And, of course, I love my clothes. That part of Posh Spice isn't an act. I do use my Gucci discount whenever I get the chance. But I'm not Posh Spice to David and he's not a famous soccer star to me. He understands the pressures and, like me, he'd rather cuddle up on the sofa watching *Blind Date* with a takeaway than be out at a club. David likes me for me. It's got nothing to do with the job I do. Most of the time we spend together we stay indoors and I wander around with no make-up and just a tracksuit on.'

Given that the two shared attitudes to their fame, just as they did about many other things, it was no surprise that, despite the fact that David and Victoria were still very young, the two were talking about getting engaged.

Jackie revealed that fact when she inadvertently blurted out, 'They're getting married, you know. Oh, I shouldn't have said anything.'

Victoria herself was the next to let slip what was happening when in Germany for the premiere of *SpiceWorld: The Movie*. 'My boyfriend is a football player,' she announced. 'We are soon getting married. As soon as Gucci makes clothes for expectant mums, I would even consider a pregnancy.'

In lieu, perhaps, of actual babies, the couple bought a pair of Rottweiler puppies, which rejoiced in the names Puff Daddy and Snoop Doggy Dogg. Christmas rolled round and with it the lavish gift giving for which the two came to be known: David gave Victoria a £13,000 jewel-studded cross and received in return an £11,000 gold and diamond bracelet.

The actual Christmas celebrations took place in a Manchester hotel and it is notable that Victoria's parents attended and David's didn't. But the two young superstars were in no mood to worry about that, for they had decided that, despite the fact that they had known one another for less than a year, they would definitely be getting married. David booked a room at the Rookery Hall Hotel in Nantwich, Cheshire, for the night of 24 January 1998, and it was here that he finally asked Victoria to be his bride. When Victoria arrived, she was presented with 30 roses and then escorted up to the room, which David had filled with red and yellow roses and lilies costing £200. The setting and the scene could not have been more romantic.

'While I was in America, we decided we would get engaged,' Victoria related afterwards. 'I told him what my dream ring would be. He remembered and had it specially designed for me. We came straight here after the game and ordered champagne and dinner in our room. We were sitting there in our dressing gowns when David pulled out the ring, got down on one knee and said, "Will you marry me Victoria?" I said yes, then produced my own ring and said, "Don't forget girl power – will you marry me?" I'd chosen the ring with my mum and dad in Los Angeles.'

Victoria's ring was a £40,000 solitaire from Boodle and Dunthorne and David's was encrusted with diamonds.

The news was made public the next day – indeed, the two staged an impromptu press conference outside the hotel – and, while no one who knew them well was surprised, just about everyone was delighted (although David's father, tellingly, had not yet heard the news when the press told him about it and he refused to comment).

David himself couldn't wait. 'Gary Neville will be my best man,' he said. 'He's my best mate and was the man who first knew how I felt about Victoria. He'll already be getting nervous about his speech. The boss will be pleased. He doesn't interfere in our private lives. He just wants me to make sure I keep myself fit and he trusts me.'

David was being wildly optimistic. Sir Alex did indeed like his boys to settle down young, believing it grounded them, but his ideal of a wife for a Manchester United player was emphatically not Victoria Adams.

But David was in love and could think about little other than the big day. 'I wasn't at all nervous about getting engaged and we decided a while ago we would make it official this weekend,' he said. 'I got the ring and was really looking forward to it. But when the moment came there were a few butterflies. It was very funny when she pulled out a ring for me. Typical. I'm ready for all the wedding talk and plans. She's already started on about dresses and even the flowers. It'll be the best day of our lives.'

The day in question, though, would not be taking place for a while yet. David and Victoria were not exactly the sort of people who would want a small-scale affair and the type of event they were thinking of needed some serious planning. And, on top of that, there were two busy schedules that needed to be taken into consideration. For David and Victoria were going to have a wedding that didn't just celebrate their nuptials: it was to be a coronation for the undoubted king and queen of Planet Celeb.

CHAPTER 3

EVERYONE LOVES A LOVER – UNLESS HE GETS A RED CARD...

The news of Victoria and David's engagement made headlines around the world. The Spice Girls were still enormously successful, ensuring that every move any of them made resulted in blanket media coverage, while David's star was also on the rise. His involvement with Victoria had raised his profile enormously, while at the same time his skill on the pitch seemed to be increasing almost by the hour. Just a couple of days after announcing his engagement, United beat Chelsea 5–3, with David scoring two of the goals. It seemed the golden boy of soccer could do no wrong.

That January, there was also a foretaste of what else was to come. David accompanied Victoria to the Versace fashion show in Milan, a clear indication of where his interests lay off the field. Indeed, all high-street wear had now been banished to the back of his wardrobe, while Gucci and Prada – also Victoria's favourites – were becoming a staple in his wardrobe. He and Victoria were also beginning to favour his and hers designer outfits, with the two of them sometimes dressed almost identically when they went out on the town.

And both were wildly excited about the engagement. 'I fell in love with David very quickly,' said Victoria. 'I knew within a couple of weeks of that first kiss. I've had boyfriends before – I've been engaged before – but it never felt like it has with David. We just work so well together and being with him feels so right. I wanted to tell the world, but I had to hold back. I wanted to be sure he felt the same way. But he did. We were at my parents' again. David told me that he loved me and I said, "I love you, too." And that was that.'

Of course, there was an awful lot at stake here. David was a high-profile professional footballer and Victoria also had her own future to consider. She was part of one of the most massively successful girl groups ever and there was concern in some quarters (not least the Spice Girls' record label) that her marriage might prompt a split in the group. Victoria was adamant that would not be the case.

'Getting married will not affect the future of the Spice Girls,' she said. 'I sat them down a few weeks ago when we were in Australia to tell them that we were getting engaged and they were all thrilled. David knows that the other girls are very, very important to me and I'm not sure I would have gone through with this if they didn't support me. Since then, we've spent all our spare time talking about the wedding. They all want to be bridesmaids and there are already arguments about what shoes they're going to wear. I asked them not to wear those huge buffalo trainers but they probably will.'

Now a seriously hot property, David also continued to attract those increasingly lucrative sponsorship deals. The latest was with Adidas, in an unprecedented seven-year £4 million arrangement. On top of that, he was earning £20,000 a week and was now worth an estimated £10 million. But this did not meet with joy from all quarters and inevitably there were some fears that all this might start going to David's head.

David was polite, but insisted that would not be the case. 'A lot has been made about me supposedly getting too big for my boots,' he said. 'But the people who know me know that isn't true. A lot of things have changed in my life – but the way I am hasn't. I have a lot of people who will knock me down if I do change. Alex Ferguson hasn't said, "Cut it out," because he doesn't think I'm doing anything wrong. He has told me I'm handling everything well. Glenn Hoddle doesn't see a problem either. And the other players don't.'

But, as his fame increased, so did the aggravation that went with it. His car was stolen and then burned, almost certainly because of the identity of its owner. Someone began stalking him and then, worse still, someone sent bullets through the post with David's name on them. It was a deeply upsetting experience and was the first of many occasions when he had to increase the security surrounding him and his family, and it may well also have been the reason that he started showing an on-field characteristic that was nearly to ruin him – a bad temper.

The first sign that David's temper might be about to cause problems came in a match against Chelsea. There was a flare-up on the pitch and David was given a yellow card. Glenn Hoddle, who was at that time England manager, was not pleased: the World Cup was only a few months away and he wanted to ensure all his team were absolutely ready for the tournament. Flare-ups on the pitch were not what he wanted at all. 'David got booked again needlessly and we have to talk,' he snapped. 'He had a similar problem for us in Le Tournoi last year and we can't afford that sort of behaviour at the World Cup finals this summer.'

David, as the world now knows, did not heed that very good advice.

However, off the pitch he seemed as grounded as ever. He might have been a megastar, but he certainly wasn't about to go all grand on the back of it. 'The other day I was round at Victoria's house and the postman rang the bell to deliver something,' he said. 'I went and answered the door and his jaw dropped. "Blimey," he said, "I never thought I'd see a legend this early in the morning." But that's just daft. I'm only 22. I haven't done anything.'

This attitude also applied to his relationship with Victoria, with Beckham insisting that it was Victoria the person rather than Victoria the star that he had fallen in love with. 'I like

Victoria for herself, not anything else,' he said. 'I'd like her if she worked in Tesco. We both understand the pressures of fame and encourage each other to ignore it or we laugh about it. She's more famous than me anyway! Some days I find four or five girls crying outside the front door. I can't understand how people get like that.'

Nor was it just sobbing girls, desperate for a glimpse of their idol. David also could not quite believe just how excited everyone got about his appearance, his life and, indeed, just him. 'It's a shame that my new hairstyle can make the front of the papers when there's so many more important things going on in the world,' he said. 'It shocks me. There's kids all over the world that are losing lives and losing families and then because I've gone blond it's on the front of the paper. It's not my fault. When I go to a restaurant, it's not because I want to go and get my picture taken, it's because I want to go and have a nice meal. I can't go to a nice restaurant in a tracksuit. I have to dress up for my picture.'

But, despite this modest attitude, flare-ups did continue on the pitch. Perhaps, in retrospect, they were the making of him, for the disastrous flare-up that was to come a few months later provoked such a furore that David has kept his temper on a very tight leash since then. The stress had been getting to him, not only in terms of dealing with his fame, but also when it came to the pressure to succeed.

'The first time I really got into the squad, the manager wasn't using me a lot,' he recalled. 'I was on the bench and sometimes I wasn't even getting changed. That kept me hungry. I always wanted to be there. And, once I got a taste for it, I felt sort of embarrassed if I wasn't there. When I got to Manchester, I didn't want people down in London saying, "Oh, he'll be back in a couple of years because he's crap. And I was worried they would also be saying that I hadn't made the standard. It was a sort of embarrassment.'

But it was also an impetus to push himself hard – and David did.

And, while most of us will never have to cope with the kind of pressure caused by mega-fame, the famous help the famous and that is what happened in the case of David. He was meeting other people who suffered from the same causes of stress and they all banded together to help each other. One person who empathised with Becks was Ronnie O'Sullivan, the snooker champion. 'It can all get too much sometimes,' he said in 1998, a statement with which David surely would have agreed. 'But I've got people to share the problems with – as well as the good times – and that helps.

'I remember meeting David Beckham in a club near where we are both from, in Chingford, three years ago. It was before he was famous. We hit it off and he would invite me up to Manchester for games of pool. The only problem was that he'd beat me – he's a right hustler. I called him just before United's semi-final against Borussia Dortmund last year and I wished him all the best. People might want to be a snooker player like me, but I want to be a footballer like David. I love watching him because he is so dangerous. He does things on the field that make you sit up and take notice, like I try to do on the snooker table.'

There were, of course, massive compensations as well, and one of them was the money. David and Victoria now made their first really significant property purchase: a £300,000 penthouse flat in Alderley Edge, Cheshire.

David also chose this moment to bring out the first of his autobiographies, entitled *My Story*. He was pretty young to be writing his life story, and this was perhaps why the book was as notable for all the pictures of him it contained as for any life experience. After all, he was still a year away from getting married.

As United fans began to absorb the figure he'd become, so they turned their attentions towards David's private life and, in particular, his bride-to-be. They had taken to singing songs about what the couple got up to after lights out, and they weren't being that complimentary. 'It's pretty difficult when you're young and you're getting that sort of stick off crowds,' said David with commendable understatement. 'It's hard to get used to. It's not as if they're saying it about your football, they're saying it about your private life. But, every time they've said it, I've gone and scored.'

Then there was that other crucial relationship in his life: that with Sir Alex Ferguson. Fergie was still some way away from reaching breaking point where David was concerned, and, despite his ongoing worries about David's superstar status, the pair remained extremely close. Not that Sir Alex was exactly a cosy figure. 'He frightens the hell out of players, but, when you have a manager for so many years, you get used to his ways,' said David. 'The best thing is, you know where you stand. If you've done terrible in a game, he'll tell you straight down the line and the next day he'll forget about it. He doesn't hold grudges. He's the best manager I've ever had. Well, he's the only manager I've ever had at this level. But he's the best manager I've ever had.'

With the World Cup looming ever closer, David and Victoria seized the chance for a quick trip to visit Sir Elton John in his pink chateau on the Cote d'Azur. The two were becoming accustomed to making headlines practically every time they went outside, but nothing could have prepared them for the fuss occasioned by one of David's new fashion items – a sarong. The two had gone out for dinner á deux at the Chevre D'Or restaurant, and, while Victoria, perhaps rather unfortunately, appeared wearing the trousers, David seemed to be wearing a skirt. That he had trousers underneath did nothing to diminish the impact of his new look: it made headlines worldwide and, when it emerged that the sarong was by Gaultier, the Gaultier shop sold out. If ever there were an object lesson in why sponsors are quite so keen to sponsor David, this was it. Not everyone thought so, of course, leading to much jeering along the lines that David was wearing a skirt, but he was defended in the most unlikely quarters.

'At Liverpool, other players used to laugh at John Barnes for wearing his fancy suits,' said Alan Hansen, speaking out in support of Becks. 'You would hear a groan go around the tour bus the minute he arrived each morning, but I thought he looked great.'

Another supporter of David's right to wear anything he chose was Chris Scott-Gray, director of the Menswear Council. 'It's great to see a footballer in something other than muddy kit or a flashy suit that doesn't suit him,' he said. 'Beckham can get away with the sarong because he is young, but clothes and style are not necessarily a youth thing. British men have never seemed to master the straightforward rules of dressing. They seem to give up once they've passed their twenties – when they dress to pull.'

That a one-off appearance could strike such a national debate was yet another sign of the phenomenon David was becoming. From here it was just one short step to icon. Except that it wasn't. The World Cup was about to begin – and it was during the tournament that a petty flash of temper very nearly cost David his career.

Indeed, the World Cup was attracting its own fair share of comment before it had even begun. There had already been uproar in some quarters when it emerged that Paul Gascoigne, who sadly had begun that long march downhill in earnest, was not going to play; now there was a second huge fuss when David's teammate Teddy Sheringham was spotted drinking while out in the Algarve.

David stood up for his teammate – and, goodness knows, he was going to need some serious support himself before too long. 'It is not my place to make any sort of judgement on Teddy – that is down to the England boss,' he said. 'But what I will say is that, knowing Teddy as I do, I have no doubt he will be up for it at the World Cup. No way, whatever has happened, whatever has been going on, will he not be totally fit and ready. I'm sure the events of the last few days will give him an even greater incentive to prove everyone wrong.'

And so the World Cup finally began. Almost immediately, it looked as if it was not going to be a good tournament for David, as indeed proved to be the case, because he simply wasn't being chosen. England's opening match was against Tunisia, and, to David's horror, he was dropped from the team. Darren Anderton replaced him. It was an awful setback, one that upset not only David, but also Sir Alex Ferguson and Sir Bobby Charlton.

'Alex Ferguson has already said that he was a little disappointed that Glenn Hoddle put David in front of his press corps and I would have to agree with that,' said Sir Bobby. 'David wants to be the best player in the world. He just knows he has so much skill and ability and I don't think he understands why he's not playing. He has an ability which isn't anywhere else in the team. His passing and ability to score goals, the quality of his crossing if he plays on the right side. You're looking at one of the rare players in the world. He's got fantastic ability.'

That was praise indeed from one of the biggest names in football, but it did nothing to cheer David up. His mood began to worsen and his friend Teddy Sheringham was now the one to offer support. 'Yes, David is very down,' he said. 'I was surprised he wasn't chosen, especially as he played in all the eight qualifiers – perhaps it's a sign of all the excellent players we have now.'

As for Hoddle himself, he was very irritable when his judgement was questioned, pointing out that England had won the match 2–0.

David continued to brood. Perhaps it was because he was now the focus of so much attention that being passed over on the pitch wounded him deeply, especially as he knew that he was now a world-class footballer. 'I have had a few days to think about it and I still don't know what went wrong,' he said, a little while after the match. 'The manager did sit down and explain a few things, but it was more of a pat on the back. I did ask him why I wasn't there but I'd rather keep the answer between us. He just sees some things different to me.'

It was a shame that Victoria wasn't there, for she and David might have been able to talk it through. But she was thousands of miles away, touring America with the Spice Girls, and so there was no one, other than his teammates, that David could really turn to. And the brooding was turning into temper, resulting in an uncharacteristic lashing out when a journalist asked if he hadn't been chosen because he had a difficult personality (for which, read 'was getting big-headed').

'There's people who don't know me as a person and they shouldn't start judging,' he snarled. 'I don't think I have done anything wrong in terms of what happens around me. Stuff goes on because people take pictures of me when I'm out. Just because I've got a famous girlfriend doesn't mean I'm up in the clouds and no one can speak to me. I didn't sulk, like a few people suggested. I didn't say much to the manager. I asked questions and he gave answers, but he did not say I wouldn't be playing again, thank goodness.

'You could argue I wasn't reproducing my usual form and I have heard it said that I dipped. Maybe in a couple of games I was tired but the manager picked me in every one that mattered and I don't think my form has been affected that much. It would have been nice to play for just ten minutes against Tunisia and I think I would have felt better had I got on. But the manager has his team and he sticks with that. In the end there's nothing I can do or say if that's his decision.'

David was clearly feeling deeply resentful and it was eating away at him. Glenn Hoddle, meanwhile, was also feeling resentful, but in his case it was because of the very public criticism levelled at him by Sir Alex Ferguson, and he lashed out at the Manchester United manager in a war of words that was rapidly becoming a sideshow to the World Cup itself. 'David was not focused coming into the tournament – he was vague – and maybe his club need to look at that further,' he remarked. 'I had a chat with him and he's more focused now but I needed to have words before that sank in. I love him to bits – after all, I brought him in. But he's got to understand that football comes first. His focus was not there but now he understands what I'm looking for.'

Nor was he happy about Ferguson's comments about David. 'Everyone is different, but I would never have put that sort of pressure on Alex Ferguson before a big European game,' he said. 'To come out with some of the things he said on the eve of a World Cup game was unprofessional. People can have their own opinions and they are welcome to them. It's a bit disappointing, but it's not just Ferguson doing it – there are other people, on TV and in newspapers.'

The pressure was clearly beginning to tell.

And then, just briefly, everything seemed to get better. First, David was brought on as a substitute in England's second match against Romania and then he played in the next game, a match against Colombia. Here he showed his true worth, scoring a goal with a free kick and thus contributing to the 2–0 win.

Then, quite suddenly – calamity struck.

With David on such good form, it made sense to play him in England's next match, against Argentina, and so he duly ran out on the field with the rest of the team. Then, just over halfway through the match, David was fouled by the Argentine captain Diego Simeone and, in a very petty display of retribution, David clipped him with his heel. Simeone collapsed theatrically to the ground, seemingly in terrible pain. It was a display that, in retrospect, was almost certainly hammed up, but it achieved its purpose and David was shown the red card and sent off, instead of merely receiving the yellow card, which was widely held to be the appropriate punishment for his crime.

From that moment, England's (and David's) fate was sealed. The remaining ten members of the team gave an outstanding performance, but the match ended 2–2, with Argentina winning 4–3 on penalties. England hadn't only lost the match: it had lost the World Cup, too. Glenn Hoddle was livid. His former warnings that David had to keep his temper under control had been proven spot on and the consequences of what he had done were immense.

'That cost us dearly,' said a grim-faced Hoddle. 'With ten men, we defended like lions. It's a bitter, bitter pill to take and we are absolutely distraught but proud at the same time. I don't know if it was destiny – everything just went against us. It's not a night for excuses, it's a night for us to be proud for England.'

Hoddle's attitude was completely understandable, but what he had failed to grasp was quite how great the backlash would be against Beckham. Others involved were not surprised. Sir Bobby Charlton, who had been in the game long enough to know exactly how the fans would react, tried to head off the furore that would ensue. 'You cannot throw him to the wolves,' he implored. 'I saw him after the match and he was terribly affected by it. He realised what he had done. I have not seen any replays but David Beckham was brought down and reacted by kicking out, for which he was given a red card.

'That came after England's great first-half performance and

it was always going to be difficult against one of the best sides in the world. Everyone knows the consequences of reacting. He's a young lad and he's paid a very high price. I know that, and he will have other World Cups where he can put that right. But it made life difficult for the rest of his team and he appreciates this, too.'

Indeed, David himself was clearly appalled by what he'd done and issued a public apology. 'This is, without doubt, the worst moment of my career and I will always regret what I did,' he said. 'I have apologised to my England teammates and manager Glenn Hoddle and I want every English supporter to know how sorry I am.'

With that, he flew to New York to be with Victoria, really the only person who could provide comfort at such a terrible time. She too begged the public to be forgiving. 'Please don't hate him,' she said. 'He doesn't deserve to be the most hated man in Britain. He, more than anyone, wanted England to go all the way. I am as upset as everyone in Britain. David needs my support. I just want to be with him. We love each other very much and it is important to get us through this.'

But none of this had any impact whatsoever. England fans and even people who had no interest in football but had been alerted by the furore as to what was going on were furious with David and they were determined to make him suffer for what he had done. And they were certainly to succeed there. David was to find himself at the centre of a campaign of vilification the likes of which had rarely been seen before.

It started innocuously enough: Adidas, one of David's sponsors, withdrew two advertisements featuring their star, saying they had 'run their course'. Then West Ham supporters had their say. West Ham were to play United in the latter's first away game of the season in August; six weeks before the match, the fans hung a threatening poster at the gates of Upton Park. Sir Alex Ferguson might have been rough on David at some points in his career, but he was certainly proving supportive now.

'We will be looking after the player and we will protect him, because that is the way Manchester United behave,' he said. 'We are a great club and we will not be giving into mob rule. I admit there are sound reasons for thinking it would make sense for David to go and play abroad, but that would be the easy way out. In any case, he doesn't want to leave Old Trafford. He's Manchester United through and through.'

But the real campaign of hatred against David was only just getting started. Ted and Sandra Beckham were also receiving abuse and had to be put under police protection. In one of the vilest moments of the persecution of Beckham, an effigy of him was hung up outside the Pleasant Pheasant pub in South Norwood, London. The police eventually insisted it was taken down. Another pub, the Horse and Groom in Islingwood, East Sussex, got in on the act: the owner, Phil Murray, filed a lawsuit against Becks over loss of earnings, claiming takings fell when England were booted out of the World Cup.

Just in case David was in any doubt as to how the fans felt about him, footballing website Football365 had its say and published a piece under the headline: IT IS OUR DUTY TO TAUNT HIM. It certainly gave David a taste of how the fans felt.

'It is our patriotic duty to give him hell verbally the next season. Relentlessly,' it thundered. 'We need to demonstrate some imagination. There is no point in just booing him all the time. He will soon get used to it. So sometimes we need a slow handclap. On other occasions, whistles or deadly silence – not a murmur from the crowd when he's in possession. When he can cope with all this and not run whinging to his agent or manager or Italy, then we will know he is up to wearing the Three Lions once more.'

By this time, it was becoming clear to some less hot-headed souls in the footballing community that the punishment was far outweighing the crime. Again, proponents of the beautiful game made an effort to defend their young star and to tell the fans that it had gone far enough. Glenn Hoddle himself made a public plea for peace. 'I hope the fans are going to be fair,' he said. 'He's reacted in a foolish way and has to understand that he can't react like that again. Why do we always need a scapegoat? He put in a fantastic performance against Colombia, but all that gets forgotten. David's had to take a bit of stick already in his career and it will be sad if that gets worse because of this, but that's the nature of our game.

'I would plead with people to look at the positive aspect of his games in an England shirt, although he's a strong enough character to take it on the chin. David is very down but we will have a chat and he's got to learn from it. We must not go overboard about it – it's not a time to blame anybody. What David did wasn't violent conduct and it shouldn't have been a red card. Then again, it was such a foolish thing to do and he has to understand he can't do those sorts of things at this level. We've been trying to drum that into him for some time but there's no blame to be put on anybody's shoulders here. He might even become a better player if he goes on to learn from this.'

Perhaps he did, for David has certainly never committed an act of similar idiocy on the field since then. But, despite the constant pleas for restraint and compassion from the game's insiders, it was to be months before David found his way back into the public's favour. Given that he is now quite possibly the best-loved man in Britain, it is easy to forget that it was very different for him then, back in the dark days of 1998.

It was a miserable time. David went around dressed all in black, with a black hat covering his hair, clearly trying to look as inconspicuous as possible. His misery was so apparent that the golfer Lee Westwood called for him to be left alone. 'It's sad when the public can't look upon sport as a game,' he said. 'At the end of the day, it is not life and death. David got sent off against Argentina and probably regrets it, but what can he do about it? When tensions are high and there's a lot of passion, you do things and sometimes you say things you don't mean. I think it is sad. Football, like golf, is just a game. You can go home and do whatever you want and forget about it and no one is hurt, are they? It's not like a war, although some people treat it like that, which is the wrong attitude.'

Even George Michael came to his support, comparing David's ordeal to his own public disgrace when he was arrested in a Beverly Hills public lavatory. 'Even though I was as pissed off with him as we all were, let's be honest, one little mistake … well, I can relate, man.'

Training began in mid-July and, for the first time in over a month, David began to look a little bit more cheerful. He was caught horsing around on the field with Teddy Sheringham: the latter pushed Beckham off the ball and David responded by flicking his right foot at him as a joke. He even managed a smile. Everyone began to relax a little and David even began to be able to walk around the streets near his home again without causing a riot.

The locals were supportive. 'I think people are rallying right behind him and are more than a little bit appalled at the abuse he has been getting,' said Kevin Meredith, who owned the local newsagent's. 'David normally comes in here every morning for his newspapers but the last couple of days he has stayed in the car while his father has fetched them.'

Even the West Ham supporters, who had been threatening David with a terrible reception, began to calm down. Shane Barber, who edits a West Ham fanzine, had been about to launch a 10,000-red-card campaign against poor Beckham, in which 10,000 supporters would wave red cards at the fallen hero, but it was called off shortly before the match. 'It won't go ahead – it's got out of hand.'

Even so, it was at this time that a move to Real Madrid was first suggested. Such was the intensity of the feelings aroused that many believed David would simply not be able to continue living in this country. But the fact was that David didn't want to go – and neither, back then, did Sir Alex Ferguson wish to lose his brilliant player. David was not, however, quite up to facing the public yet: he pulled out of a friendly against Birmingham. His England teammate Gareth Southgate, who had himself been the recipient of venom from the fans when he missed in a penalty shootout against Germany in the semi-final of Euro '96, warned David that he would just have to take it.

'The next few weeks are not going to be very nice for David,' he said. 'The poor lad has already gone through far more than I ever suffered, but I can still give him some good advice because of my own experience. I took a lot of stick, including verbal abuse, nasty letters and people crossing the road to avoid me. The way you deal with it is the important thing and I was determined to stand up, be a man and try to explain to all those critics that football is merely a game.

'Eventually, the tide turned for me. Most people were sympathetic and I am certain this will be the case for David as well. I have every confidence he can win this battle, even though it is going to be hard for him – very, very hard. David seems a quiet lad, yet I have no doubt he possesses the character and personality to come out the other side. He wouldn't have progressed as far as he has in the game without a lot of inner strength. None of the England players blame David. We should never have been forced to take on Argentina in the second round, because other things could have been done by the management to avoid that fixture. David has been made a scapegoat. The public have reacted entirely wrongly. Incidents such as his effigy being hung from a lamp-post are utterly disgusting.'

David must have been enormously heartened by those words and even more so when he played in a friendly in Oslo against part-timers Valerenga. It was his first game since the match against Argentina and he was given a hero's welcome, with 20,000 fans roaring their approval as the teams were read out. Even before the match began, the fans were determined to tell David he was out of the wilderness: he was presented with a Player of the Year trophy by the Norwegian branch of the United fan club.

It was the perfect setting for David to make his first appearance and it showed. For the first time the haunted look he had been wearing for the past seven weeks began to slip and his joy in acknowledging the fans spoke for itself. The only fly in the ointment was that he sprained his ankle and so was forced to miss out a friendly a couple of days later with Danish side Brondby – but, given his new status as the returned prodigal son, it was a small price to pay.

A sure sign that David was being forgiven came when

people began to joke about what he had done. An Internet site posted a game in which players scored if they made a virtual David foul rival players – and scored even more if they managed to do so as a cartoon figure of Victoria flashed her knickers. It was childish – and exactly what the country needed to put recent events into perspective.

There were still rumblings from some quarters, not least when United played Arsenal at Wembley and rival fans gave David to understand that they had not been pleased with his actions, but they were increasingly muted. United itself could not have been more supportive, not least when, in mid-August, David signed a new five-year £6 million contract with the club. Fears that he might leave the country had been proved wrong. 'I'm delighted to commit myself to the club long-term,' he said. 'This is where I grew up and where I want to stay. It's a great start to the new season for me because it's a special club with some very special players.'

Alex Ferguson also expressed his delight. 'I am really pleased,' he said. 'This obviously confirms United's intentions to have all of their major players signed on long-term deals. It speaks very highly of our players' commitment to the club and United's commitment to them and their futures.'

The shows of support were becoming increasingly public as David worked – or rather, played – his way back into the nation's heart. United played Leicester at Old Trafford, resulting in a 2–2 draw, with David scoring one of the goals. Some members of the crowd had been booing but the majority were in support, something acknowledged by David as he raised his right fist in tribute. He was publicly embraced on the field both by United's assistant manager Brian Kidd and by Leicester's Robbie Savage, a friend of David's and someone who had played with him in United's Youth team. Savage did, however, warn that it was not over yet. 'I'm afraid this is going to go on for months,' he said. 'David has to go to West Ham next week, when it will be different again. And I suspect that, when United come to Leicester, he'll still be getting some stick.'

Indeed, that West Ham match was seen as something of a potential crisis point for the player – it was, after all, West Ham fans who had been planning the red-card protest. But then, a couple of things happened to divert everyone's attention – and they both, needless to say, involved Victoria. The Spice Girls were still on tour in the United States, where they posed for a sensational photo shoot for the gay magazine *Attitude*, dressing up as members of the camp 1970s band Village People. In the accompanying interview Victoria revealed quite how famous she and David had become as a couple, when she recounted a meeting with Madonna at which David was present. 'She was acting like she knew us,' said a slightly overawed Posh. 'I said, "This is my boyfriend," and she said, "Yes. You're the footballer." He was saying, "I can't believe Madonna knows who I am."'

But far, far more significant than that was the revelation that Victoria was three months pregnant. That time in the South of France had clearly proved fruitful and David and

Victoria, both of whom were keen to start a family, were thrilled. 'I'm absolutely delighted,' said Victoria, speaking publicly for the first time about the baby. 'The baby wasn't planned but I never for one moment considered not keeping it. Why would I? I love David, we are getting married and would have had children fairly soon anyway. I kept the pregnancy quiet just in case something went wrong. But I'm over three months now and I don't mind everyone knowing how happy I am.'

After all the drama of the summer, there could have been nothing better to cheer up David again – and to take his mind off that forthcoming match.

Indeed, Victoria related quite how overwhelmed David had been when she revealed the good news. 'When I told David I was pregnant, he just started weeping,' she said. 'He must have cried for about an hour and I had tears running down my face, too. It was a very emotional moment for both of us. The baby wasn't planned so it was a surprise mixed with real delight. I think telling David he was going to be a dad really put things in perspective for him because I know he's had such a hard year professionally.'

As if one Spice pregnancy wasn't enough, Mel B then revealed that she, too, was pregnant by the dancer Jimmy Gulzar, and was going to step up the aisle with him before the baby was born. It was very nearly a case of dancing in the streets – except at the girls' record company, that is, where bosses were said not to be holding celebrations about the news.

David, however, was still saying nothing publicly. That dreaded West Ham match was finally upon him and a mob of about 500 fans behaved appallingly, signalling that they, at least, had not forgiven him. David was pelted with stones and hit with a beer glass as the crowd booed and jeered him, and his good news. And their fury was not solely because of the World Cup: many were enraged that a player from east London should be part of the United team. David behaved magnificently: he rose above it all, said nothing and got on with the game, which resulted in a 0–0 draw. The crowd finally fell silent and David was able to leave the match with his dignity – and all his bones – intact.

That match really did signal an end to the hostilities. David had clearly suffered badly through anguish and remorse; he had endured a display of vitriolic hatred quite out of proportion to anything he had done – and now, as a father-to-be, he was ready to move on.

Victoria finally returned to England in September and, with David, made her first public appearance – fittingly enough – at the christening of her sister Louise's daughter Liberty. All the Spice Girls were clearly revelling in the situation. Mel B told Radio 1 that she and Victoria 'turned into dragons. It was kinda funny'. Meanwhile, Victoria said of her pregnancy, 'It's something we all look forward to. It's only natural. We've all said having a family was something we wanted.'

Being back in England did have a downside, though. So much had happened since Victoria had gone away – David's red card and its aftermath, and her pregnancy – that photographers were even more desperate than usual to capture pictures of the couple. This led to a nasty incident at a service station on the motorway. Victoria and the girls had been playing at a concert in Sheffield, after which she and David were driven back to his home in Cheshire in a chauffeured Mercedes. Once on the M62 they noticed a car following them, and so the car sped up before pulling up at a service station. Their pursuer, a photographer, tried to take pictures of Victoria, who was apparently wearing a dressing gown, at which point David got into a fight with the man and the police were called.

'It was beyond belief. It really was a devilish experience,' a tearful Victoria said later. 'We accept we will be photographed but there is a lot of difference between that and pursuing someone like you are on a foxhunt. The whole incident left me shaken and very upset. I truly feared for my unborn baby.'

The police were extremely sympathetic. 'It was quite frightening for Victoria, especially as she is expecting a baby,' said a spokesman. 'They were chased for some time and when they pulled up to get some petrol he tried to take a picture of Victoria. She had got changed and was trying to relax. She was wearing her dressing gown. David was very angry and they had an argument. The police were called. It did get quite serious. Both parties were spoken to and no further action will be taken.'

As the couple revelled in being together again, David

continued to redeem himself on the field. Playing against Barcelona in late September, David delivered one of his wonder goals, which drew praise not only from Glenn Hoddle but even Barcelona's goalkeeper, the Dutch Ruud Hesp. 'I knew where it was going once he struck it, but he has such a brilliant ability in these situations that there was no easy way to get to the ball,' he said. 'If he catches it right, I doubt there is any goalkeeper in the world who can stop him. People might say, if you know where it's going why doesn't the keeper move further over? But, if you go too far, he'd spot that and hit it into the opposite corner.'

It was not only business as usual as far as football was concerned: David's interest in fashion had flared up again, too. He and Victoria attended Antonio Berardi's catwalk show during London Fashion Week and were mobbed by an enthusiastic crowd shortly afterwards.

But yet more drama was in store. It was not only rogue photographers who were out to cause trouble; 'glamour models' were out to do their bit, too. And so it was that one Sunday in October a newspaper ran a shocking story, alleging that David had kissed and flirted with Page 3 girl Emma Ryan and even suggested they get a hotel room before deciding he couldn't go through with it because of his love for Victoria. It was complete nonsense and the pair laughed it off publicly, although Victoria later wrote in her autobiography about the pain it had caused. It also provoked more claims from another woman that were to prove unfounded.

It was an uncomfortable time in what had been an extraordinary year. Ever since they first got together, people had been asking of the couple, were they really so genuinely in love? The answer is yes, but, in a rather ugly display of Schadenfreude, there was a certain degree of delight from some quarters that the perfect couple were not all they seemed. As a matter of fact they were, but it caused some unhappiness for Victoria at the time. Ultimately, however, it was to draw the two yet closer together.

As the tumultuous year drew to a close, David continued to play ever better as well as fitting in a short break with Victoria in Marbella, where he was seen publicly kissing Victoria's tummy. And the show ran on much as before. David continued to experiment with new looks – a beard made an appearance in November – and continued to sign lucrative sponsorship deals, the latest being with Pepsi. There was another brief moment when it looked as if David was allowing his temper to run riot again during a clash with Blackburn skipper Tim Sherwood, but David had finally learned his lesson and the fracas was a one-off.

And by the end of the year Beckham had finally regained his footballing crown – and was the better player for it. That which does not destroy us makes us stronger and David had been through a patch that would have brought down a lesser man. However, his innate maturity, so much in evidence when he was younger, combined with the strength of his relationship with Victoria, saved him from the abyss. David had emerged a stronger man.

'There is no way I could have survived the World Cup aftermath without Victoria,' he said. 'That's why I went straight to New York to be with her. She didn't say a word when I saw her, just gave me a big cuddle. She was about a month pregnant – no one knew except us – and was as pleased to see me as I was to see her. No way did I expect things to turn as nasty as they did but, once I was with her, I knew I'd get through it.'

Eventful as this year had been, the next was to be equally full of drama. David was to become a father and a husband, in that order, and celebrate a wedding that overshadowed even that of Prince Edward and Sophie Rhys-Jones. But it was not all to be plain sailing for, as David's fame and popularity was to soar ever higher, one man was increasingly dismayed by the turn of events. That man was Sir Alex Ferguson.

CHAPTER 4

SUPER BECKS

It was a typical Beckham start to the new year: David celebrated the arrival of 1999 by buying a new £150,000 silver Ferrari 550 Maranello. It was a beautiful car, fit for a famous footballer – although, as onlookers observed, it was a two-seater with nowhere to store the nappies. No matter, David had come through a very difficult year and clearly felt he deserved a little present to cheer himself up.

He was playing well, with no major upsets, but there did seem to be a slight change in his lifestyle. Beckham had always loved clothes and revelled in being a fashion icon but, now more than ever, he seemed to be entering into Victoria's world. The two were pictured for *Vogue*, lying entwined around each other and with Victoria's seven-month bump clearly visible. Victoria gave an interview to accompany the pictures, in which she said she would carry on working after the baby's birth in March. 'I'll just take the baby straight into the studio with me.' And what would she do at night? 'Straight in a cot, although I have heard there are some babies who never sleep … aren't there?' The couple were in for a rude awakening.

The interview gave a very revealing portrait of a very close couple, with Victoria expressing herself in her usual, inimitable way. Explaining that she nearly had his and hers loos put in the master bedroom she continued, 'I've weed in front of David right from the beginning, but then we've always been more like friends. Well, looks aren't going to last forever, are they?'

It got better. Reminded that the in your face TV pundit Jeremy Clarkson had said he'd like to get David alone in a padded cell after the World Cup fiasco, Victoria mused, 'A lot of people would have topped themselves over that.' She gave David a hug. 'But don't worry, I'll look after you. Just send him round here, *I'll* beat him up.'

She was clearly on superb form, describing the Alderley Edge apartment's decor as 'a cross between a poof's house and a whore house'. Life consisted of walking the dog and snuggling up on the sofa to watch *Friends* and the two even went to the local Tesco. 'It's fine. They're very posh round where we live,' said Posh. 'If anyone wants an autograph I say, "Not until we're finished," and then I get all the children to line up and tell them that if they don't say please they're not going to get one. David and I were talking about this the other day, weren't we? We want children who are very well behaved.' It was Victoria – and David – down to a T.

To mark Valentine's Day, David gave Victoria a picture of the couple embracing: Victoria was so thrilled that she promptly ordered another one for the nursery. David then went on record to address Glenn Hoddle's accusation, namely that he was not sufficiently focused on the game.

'Personally, I didn't agree with that comment about me not being focused,' he said. 'I've been brought up to believe that, whether you're playing on Hackney Marshes or in the World Cup, you give it everything you've got. My dad, my Sunday league managers – especially one called Stewart Underwood almost 20 years ago – and now Alex Ferguson have always stressed that to me. I don't start focusing when the whistle goes, I start on the Wednesday before Saturday's match or sooner.'

The wounds from that shattering time had clearly not entirely healed. 'It was frustrating not to play in the first two games when I was so keen to do my best for my country,' he went on. 'My feelings never seemed to matter. I want to stress that I'm always happy to respect a manager's wishes but I was very keyed up by the time I got to play and I think things might have turned out differently if I'd played in those two games.' It was the closest David had ever got to blaming Glenn Hoddle for the whole debacle.

David was also keen to clarify his attitude towards his own celebrity. 'I can see how the public or football fans might think I'm letting things slip or getting distracted by celebrity nonsense but what they don't understand is that I can't step out of the front door without getting photographed – and what happens in 10 seconds of my life can stay in the papers for a month,' he said. 'I'm not flash. I like nice things and a nice lifestyle – not because they portray an image to the outside world but because they make me happy. But nothing distracts me from my football.'

He talked avidly of his happiness with Victoria. 'I've got the girl of my dreams, the job I always wanted, a baby on the way and marriage round the corner,' he said. 'There are so many good things in my life that the black moments never last long. All the criticism can fly straight over my head if I've got her to come home to. I started thinking about proposing to her about a week after we met. She came on to me, actually, but I'd had a funny feeling about Victoria before I'd even met her. I saw her on the telly and thought that, if I could just meet her once, we'd be together forever.

'I'm totally ready for fatherhood. I'm so over the moon I'm lost for words. The happiest moment of my life was when she told me she was pregnant and, although it wasn't planned, there wasn't a split second of doubt in my mind. We both understand what it involves and we're both ready for the responsibility – but then we'd better be, it's due in three weeks. I know a lot of things have been said about us being too young and not married, and being bad role models for young people. But we love each other, we're best friends and we're ready to be parents. I think that's a good example to set.'

The subject of David's football career arose and it makes ironic reading now. 'I have no great desire to play abroad, but you can never say never,' he said. 'United might get sick of me and sell me abroad or to London, but I want to stay at United for the rest of my career and continue to repay the debt I owe to the boss, the club and the best fans in the world. After that, management holds no appeal for me. What I would really like to do is open a school of excellence for kids – boys *and* girls. It's not a normal ambition for a footballer but it's something I've always wanted to do. A lot of people helped me to get where I am and I want to put something tangible back into the game.'

Did Beckham really say 'girls'? 'It's something I feel strongly about,' said David, going into full new-man mode. 'I think it's important to remove the idea that football is an exclusively male domain. When I was at school, some of the girls were as good as the boys and getting them involved more might help to remove some of the macho nonsense that mars the game.'

Sir Alex's reaction to that is not on record – but it can certainly be imagined.

As David prepared for fatherhood, there was another ordeal to be faced – Diego Simeone, the player whose antics got David sent off in the World Cup. The two were to meet at Old Trafford when Simeone's team, Inter Milan, came to play at Old Trafford and it was a reunion that was expected to be tense. Simeone attempted to extend an olive branch before the match. 'I want to make it known that I respect David Beckham and all of his Manchester United teammates,' he said. 'I have a lot of admiration for him as a footballer. He is a fantastic player. One of United's greatest strengths is their crosses, and Beckham and Ryan Giggs can pose problems for any fullback. They test the best defences.

'It is not for David Beckham to feel guilty over his sending off at the World Cup and what happened after it. This is football – the same thing has happened to me. The referee believes you have done something wrong and you must go off. I know what has been said but these are the facts: Argentina won the match against England because we beat them in a penalty shootout. That is all, no other reason. Such a thing can not be the fault of one player. As far as I am concerned, our duel is history. That was the World Cup and this is the Champions League and Inter is all that matters to me now.'

David did not reply.

Simeone made matters still worse when he confessed to overreacting during the match. 'Let's just say the referee fell into the trap,' he told an Italian newspaper. 'It was difficult for him because I went down well and, in moments like that, there's lots of tension. My falling transformed a yellow card into a red card. In reality, it wasn't a violent blow, it was just a little kick back with no force behind it.' These were words that were scarcely likely to endear him to United fans – let alone to David himself.

David got his revenge. United beat Inter Milan 2–0, with David setting up Dwight Yorke for the two goals. Alex Ferguson was delighted. 'Beckham is back to his best,' he said. 'They could not handle him or Dwight Yorke. I didn't say anything to David about Simeone before he went out. I didn't need to. I think he is an outstanding central midfield player. But he is also the best crosser of a ball in Europe. And, until I find someone who can cross a ball as well, he will stay out on the right.'

David, meanwhile, was gracious in his triumph. He and Simeone actually embraced and exchanged shirts before David went to acknowledge the rapture from the crowd.

One of the fans watching was Simply Red star Mick Hucknall, who was fulsome in his praise for David after the game. 'I only ever really deal with the media when I've got a new album,' he said. 'David is under much more pressure than I ever am, and I can only admire him for the way he deals with it. After the Argentina game it could all have gone horribly wrong for him. Some of the chants, the things rival fans were saying to him were appalling. Even now some of them still boo him. But he has adopted the right attitude. He is set a great example by Alex, who handles everything so professionally.

'But he still deserves a great deal of credit for the way he has focused any anger and frustration on to football. Last night I was so impressed by the way he performed. Not only did he provide two brilliant crosses but he was also defending and tackling. He was all over the park. My respect for David went up tenfold for the commitment he showed and the gesture he made by swapping shirts with Simeone. It was brilliant and showed real maturity.'

It was a fitting end to the drama and, as if to acknowledge a new beginning, Victoria went into labour the very next day.

She was taken to London's Portland Hospital where, on 4 March 1999, she gave birth to the couple's first child, a 7lb boy named Brooklyn Joseph Beckham. He was called Brooklyn because that's where Victoria was when she found she was pregnant, while Joseph is both David's middle name and the name of one of his grandfathers.

David was absolutely delighted. 'Victoria is very well,' he told assembled reporters outside the hospital. 'She is sitting up drinking champagne. I'm feeling very well, I'm over the moon – it is something I have always wanted to do. It's a new experience for me. It's the best thing that's ever happened to me. It's unbelievable – it's something that can't be beaten. The birth was natural and there were no complications, nothing at all. Victoria might be here for a couple more days.'

A succession of visitors included Emma Bunton and Victoria's parents and brother and sister, while Spice Girls fans kept vigil outside the hospital. It then emerged that, in fact, there had been a slight complication – Victoria was forced to have a Caesarean when doctors discovered that Brooklyn was in the wrong position. But it was a time of great rejoicing for David and the start of a period that was going to turn him into possibly the most famous father in Britain.

Victoria stayed in the hospital for five days, after which the new family made a getaway in true Hollywood style. A limousine with blacked-out windows pulled up at the Portland's goods entrance, Victoria and David clambered inside with Brooklyn and the car roared off with a police escort to Victoria's parents' home in Goff's Oak. Later, David emerged to make a statement: 'We just want to be on our own, just the three of us,' he said. 'The baby is lovely, sitting in his mum's arms. I am very pleased. Victoria's fine, naturally she's a bit tired, but she's sitting with him in her arms – it's great.'

Other family members also spoke of their happiness. Victoria's sister Louise said, 'He's fast asleep. It's lovely to have them home and Victoria's so pleased to be back with her family.'

Meanwhile, Jackie Adams, Victoria's mother, said, 'The baby is lovely. It's good to be a grandma.'

It is noteworthy, though, that David's parents weren't there. They had been present at the hospital when Victoria gave birth and had already seen their new grandson, but it was with her own parents that Victoria chose to spend the following weeks. From the very earliest days that David and Victoria were together, their life outside football tended to revolve around her parents rather than his. The Adams family spoke warmly about welcoming David into their midst, but in doing so it is possible that David's parents felt left out.

Logistically, it made sense for the couple to spend their time at Goff's Oak, for the simple reason that Victoria's parents were better off than David's and thus had a bigger house, but, even so, a picture was beginning to emerge. David was entering Victoria's world rather than vice versa and it was to lead to David's father Ted talking with some regret about growing apart from his famous son.

With his home life so secure, David was beginning to put

the events of the past year into perspective. Glenn Hoddle had recently published an account of the World Cup, in which he revealed that he ignored David after the game, believing it would be best to leave him alone – a decision that David found deeply wounding. 'When I was shown the red card, I was really gutted,' he said. 'More than anything I wanted to play the rest of the game. That was the only thing I was really thinking about – and the team winning, of course.

'I was sat outside the changing room afterwards when Tony Adams came over. He sat down with me and he was brilliant. I will remember that because that was what I needed at the time. The manager didn't actually speak to me after the game. Not at all. My family and friends were the only people who wanted to talk to me.'

But David conceded that he had learned a great deal from the whole experience. 'It made me grow up a lot,' he said. 'It has made me realise a few things, although I feel that with everything that happened after the World Cup I was treated unfairly. I think the majority [of fans] dislike me. I don't know whether it's jealousy or not, but I think there are more people who don't like me than like me. I'd like to be really popular, but I don't think that is going to happen now.' David was being overly modest. While there would always be fans who would heckle him – probably because they were jealous – the public as a whole was beginning to warm to him as never before.

And what could be better to celebrate Brooklyn's birth than winning a high-profile match? United beat Chelsea 2–0 a few days later, and while both goals were scored by Dwight Yorke, he paid tribute to David after the first one by making a baby-rocking sign with his arms. David was delighted – and later revealed that he'd been a little weary before the match, due to baby-watching duties. 'I was a little bit tired on the morning of the match because I was up all night with him,' he confessed. 'But I had a good sleep at the hotel in the afternoon and I enjoyed the game.'

Despite David's public comments about the hurt he'd felt at the hands of Glenn Hoddle, the England manager was also generous in his praise. 'He's got good support around him and it's not only good to see him playing excellently, but also that his family life's going well, too,' he said. 'If people leave him alone, I'm sure he's going to go from strength to strength.'

Brooklyn made his first public appearance, fittingly enough, on Mother's Day. Ten days after the birth, David, Victoria, Brooklyn and the entire Adams family, plus Louise's daughter Liberty, went out en masse to celebrate at the Down Hall Country House Hotel in Bishop's Stortford. Victoria was clearly regaining her figure – in fact, the world had seen the last of the more rounded Victoria of the Spice days as she was to go on to lose an enormous amount of weight - and was looking svelte. 'I'm really happy to be with my family and a great time was had by all,' she said as the group left the restaurant. Motherhood was clearly suiting her.

Ferguson, though, was leaving David in no doubt that he was expected to carry on as usual. Despite admitting to tiredness, he played in all five of United's matches in the two weeks after Brooklyn's birth and by the time the team played Everton in late July he was beginning to look exhausted. However, he pulled himself together in the second half, scoring a magnificent goal and leading his team on to a 3–1 victory. Even Sir Alex was impressed.

The couple were clearly weary, but they were determined to bring Brooklyn up without extra help. On top of that, David was new man incarnate. 'We had a child so we can raise him, not a nanny,' said Beckham. 'I love looking after Brooklyn. In fact, I've just changed a nappy. We both get up with him in the night and Victoria's really good with Brooklyn, very motherly. She never leaves his side and she feeds him and washes his clothes – that's the way she wants it.

'We're a family now and I'm the happiest I've been in a long time. Since we've had Brooklyn, I've grown up a lot and he's made me look at life from a new perspective. If something winds me up at work I come home and take a look at what we've made together. Things that were important before just don't seem as important now. I cried when he was born. I wanted to cut his umbilical cord, but the doctor did it so quickly I didn't get the chance. He's got Victoria's nose and colouring but he's starting to go blond like me. He's got my legs, my feet and my toes – exactly the same toes as me.'

And David went on to reveal that he frequently drove through the night after matches to get back to his wife-to-be and child, and sped back to them after a recent match. 'I was tired but I hate being away from them,' he said. 'I absolutely hate it. It was 3am when I got there but I was quite happy to sit up all night just watching Brooklyn breathe. He's beautiful – different every day. He eats unbelievably, so he's gaining weight all the time. And he has started smiling, too – especially when he's got wind!'

Brooklyn was already being introduced to his parents' lifestyle. He was taken to a shopping centre by Victoria about three weeks after he was born and was spotted at London's exclusive restaurant The Ivy, dining in the company of Sir Elton John, no less. There was some amusement over his parents' appearance, given that they were still coping without a nanny: both appeared to be sleepwalking.

But, be that as it may, both were also deliriously happy. 'We'd like a couple more,' said David. 'But I don't think I'd be able to fit any more names on my football boots. I usually have Beckham printed on the front of my boot, but now it's Brooklyn, with Beckham at the back. I think the sponsors Adidas are quite pleased.' He was quoted in an interview with *Time Out* magazine, the front cover of which caused quite a stir in itself. David was pictured on the cover wearing all white, with a rosary around his neck and his arms out in a supplicating pose. The cover was entitled, 'The Resurrection Of David Beckham'. The image would have been controversial at any time, but, given that it was in the run-up to Easter, Church leaders were not best pleased.

'I think everybody has to be careful playing with symbols

that are important to other people,' said a spokesman for the United Reform Church. 'These things shouldn't be walked all over.'

Meanwhile, the Church of England's director of communications, Dr Bill Beaver, said it was 'unfortunate' that Beckham should allow himself to be pictured thus.

Meanwhile, David and Victoria were beginning to prepare for their summer wedding. After months of indecision, the two finally decided to marry in Ireland, at a spectacular venue called Luttrellstown Castle. The venue was just outside Dublin and the ceremony, which was to be covered by *OK! Magazine* in a £1-million deal, was to take place on 4 July, exactly four months after Brooklyn's birth.

Wedding invitations were sent out featuring a crest of arms, which the two had chosen for themselves – and which provoked some snorts of mirth from heraldry experts. Neither could have cared less. Victoria gave an interview to *OK!*, in which she talked about her happiness. 'All I was interested in was having a healthy baby,' she said. 'It's just amazing how much you can love another person.'

David, meanwhile, was still brooding on the pain of separation. 'It's really hard being away from the baby,' he said. 'I just want to spend every minute of the day with him. You want to be there, you want to see every little movement, every little thing that he does differently.'

As the wedding preparations continued, there was intense speculation as to whether Geri Halliwell would be invited.

David and Victoria had seen her briefly when they all had dinner in the South of France, but relations between the remaining Spice Girls and the one who walked out had become increasingly strained. In the event, there was no invitation. 'I don't even want to comment on how I feel about it,' snapped Geri at a press conference.

Victoria, meanwhile, was claiming that hardly anyone would be invited. 'David and I haven't got that many friends. We could have our wedding in a postbox if we wanted to,' she joked to Zoe Ball on Radio 1.

There was also an enormous amount of curiosity about the wedding dress. Victoria stayed coy. 'I went with Mum [to try the dress on] and we were all girlie and it was great,' she said. 'It isn't a Versace dress, there's been a lot of rumours and it isn't.'

In the run-up to the big day, David and Victoria gave an interview to *OK! Magazine*, which took place in their Cheshire flat. The flat itself was pretty much what you would expect from a Spice Girl and a footballer. There was a huge portrait of the couple by Jurgen Teller hanging in their entrance hall, and high church candles on either side of the door. The rest of the flat was also littered with candles. The kitchen was home to a fake leopard-print scatter rug, radiators shaped like ladders and a huge Miele oven; the bathroom housed an enormous bath, double shower and matching his and hers Versace robes and towels; and in the sitting room there was a four-foot elephant, side tables and a collection of

Buddhas and other statues. There were wooden floors throughout and white painted walls, covered with photographs of the couple.

The two were clearly blissfully happy and spoke openly about Brooklyn's birth and their life together. Talking about her dash to hospital, Victoria said, 'Basically, the baby's head was not in place and it would never have been, so I had a Caesarean, which was very last minute. You have a choice – you can go into labour, but if the head still doesn't engage, you end up having an emergency Caesarean, which can make the baby stressed.

'All I was interested in was having a healthy baby, and it's funny how suddenly your mind begins to work and all your priorities change. It was like when I was actually in the theatre, I said to David, "If they take the baby away, for whatever reason, just leave me here, half-dead or whatever, and just go with the baby – make sure you don't let him out of your sight." But all the doctors were absolutely fantastic, the hospital, the staff ... Mr Gillard, who actually delivered Brooklyn, was amazing and you can't even see my scar!'

Was David there? 'I couldn't watch the actual operation,' he revealed, 'but Mr Gillard said, "The head's halfway out if you want to look now," and, just as I looked up, he was pulling Brooklyn's head out, he opened his eyes ... unbelievable! I just cried.' Did his father offer advice? 'He's not really like that, my dad,' David continued. 'All we talk about is football! No, a couple of nights before Brooklyn was born he did take me to one side and said, you know, when the baby's born, when you first set eyes on him, you'll understand how we feel about you. And my mum absolutely loves babies, so she just couldn't wait.'

David was also asked if his parents were advising him to slow down a bit. 'No!' he replied. 'My mum and dad know Brooklyn and Victoria are the most important things in my life – but they also know how dedicated I am to playing football and to Manchester United.' And, it was pointed out, David put a lot of work into his relationship, while working in a field not known for its sensitivity. 'There's other working environments where people have that reputation, too,' said David calmly. 'The fact is that this is the first time I've ever been in love. I think, once you meet that person you want to spend the rest of your life with, you know and, no matter what else is going on around you, you dedicate your life to that person. You'd never hurt or destroy that relationship.'

A couple of days later, Victoria celebrated her 25th birthday by taking Brooklyn to watch United playing Sheffield – only for David to be left on the bench. But Brooklyn had now seen his father's working environment – something that he was destined to do a great deal more. 'I really wanted Brooklyn to see his dad play but he seemed to enjoy the noise and the atmosphere afterwards,' he said. 'I'm sure that he'll be coming back for more now that he's got his first game out of the way.' He might also have enjoyed the sight of 'Happy Birthday Victoria' flashing across the scoreboard.

Nothing was too much for David to do to show his devotion

to his newborn son. He had the name 'Brooklyn' tattooed along the lower half of his back, although it must be said that, should the couple turn out to have a large family, there probably won't be room for many more.

There was a brief health scare when Victoria discovered a lump in Brooklyn's stomach when she was changing him, but it turned out to be an umbilical hernia that had to be removed. 'It's a routine op and the doctors have said not to worry,' said a spokeswoman for Victoria. 'Any new parents are concerned if they have to take their baby to hospital. But David and Victoria have been assured that it's a common operation.'

Brooklyn safely returned to health and with David newly named by *France Football* magazine as the second-highest-paid footballer in the world after Ronaldo – Becks was now estimated to be earning £3 million a year – everything in the garden should have been rosy. But, as ever, there were rumblings of discontent in the background. For a start, rumours continued that Victoria was not happy living in the north and that she wanted David to move to another football team. Victoria denied it, but the couple still admitted that their Cheshire home was not permanent and that they were looking to buy a whole house in the south.

And, as ever, there was the constant worry about whether Sir Alex was still happy with his protégé. Brooklyn's birth had only intensified interest in the couple, on top of which David's publicity was now being looked after by Outside Organisation. These were the Spice Girls' agents and it was at Victoria's behest that David put his business with them. Sir Alex was saying nothing – for now.

As for David and Victoria, they didn't have time to worry, for they had something much more interesting on their agenda. They had a summer wedding to plan.

CHAPTER 5

THE BECKS A MAN CAN GET

Preparations for the wedding were now in full swing. Luttrellstown Castle found itself at the centre of attention, to the extent that security guards were employed to prevent curious fans sneaking in to find out what was going on. The castle itself boasted 14 bedrooms, reception rooms including the Van Stry Room, named after the Dutch painter and adorned with his paintings, and a dining room called the Kentian room. It had a ceiling painted in 1753 by Jacob de Wit of The Triumph of Bacchus and Ceres.

David turned 24 in May and celebrated with a quiet party at the couple's Cheshire home. Shortly afterwards he assured fans for the umpteenth time that he had no plans to quit United. 'I never had any doubts about staying,' he said. 'I think, at the start of the season, a lot of people were wondering whether I would crack. Or whether I would go abroad. But all

I wanted was to come back to United and to be playing again. That was important for me. The manager told me, "As long as you get back here and get playing for us again, then you will be fine." And I have been pleased by the way it's gone for me since then.

'At times it has been hard getting that reaction from the crowds, but the lads here have been brilliant for me. I couldn't have asked for more support. And I never had any doubts about staying. I knew I was going to get stick when I went to away grounds. I've had that every away game. But I'm playing for the biggest club in the world so I expect that. You learn as you go along and it makes you a much stronger person.' The wounds of the previous year, although healing, were still clearly not entirely cured.

Victoria, meanwhile, launched an appeal for the Meningitis Research Foundation in London. Having just had a health scare with Brooklyn, by now nine weeks old, she was increasingly aware of the fears faced by new parents, and admitted to being constantly worried about Brooklyn. 'Brooklyn is the most important thing in the world to us,' she said. 'The thought of anything happening to him is a complete nightmare. I wake up in the night in a panic. I don't know what I think might have happened to him, but I love him so much. Until you're a mother, you don't know how hard it all is.'

Brooklyn, she said had, recovered 'brilliantly' from his recent operation. 'He's fine,' she went on. 'He smiles a lot and is aware of everything around him. We're going to be like the Waltons and have a house full of children and dogs. I definitely want to have a lot more children now that I've had him. We take it in turns to do everything, he [David] bathes Brooklyn as much as I do.'

Finally, after months of speculation, Victoria's choice of wedding-dress designer was revealed: Vera Wang. The American-based designer was a surprise choice, but she certainly had form when it came to dressing celebrities, numbering Sharon Stone and Mariah Carey among her clients. 'I'd seen her work previously – other celebrities she'd dressed – and I'd always really respected her,' said Victoria.

'But I thought she was such a nice lady, open to ideas, which I think is important. There are certain little things I'd like to put on the dress and she's really open to that. I couldn't work with anyone who's got a big ego and won't listen to anyone else's opinion. It is an exciting time when you are planning a wedding and it is nice to have people who are excited about it as well.'

David was equally excited about the wedding and was also resigned to the fact that he was still hero or zero, depending on who you talked to. As United prepared for their FA Cup Final against Newcastle and the European Champions Cup Final against Bayern Munich, he revealed that he had only recently seen pictures of the effigy that had been hung outside the pub. 'I only saw a picture about four months ago,' he said. 'A grown man doing something like that is pathetic. I knew the United fans would be behind me and I think I'm playing more consistently for my club and my country.

'But you see the papers and what people are saying on the telly,' he continued, sounding slightly more aggrieved than usual. 'One minute they wanna hang you, the next you're gonna win the game against Luxembourg – my "comeback game". There's never been a point where I thought, "Right, I've won them over", because I don't think I ever will. The papers are probably writing nicer things about me, but there's still time in my career for them to change their minds again!'

His personal feelings certainly didn't affect his football. United won the FA Cup final against Newcastle, with Ferguson singling out David for praise, after which they went on to trounce Bayern Munich. The club was now being spoken of as one of the greatest ever, with Beckham in particular increasingly being cited as a truly great footballer. Such was his prowess that the fans were even prepared to overlook his new-mannishness, his frequent declarations of love for Victoria and Brooklyn, his modelling sessions and his love of fashion.

Even more unusually for a footballer, David was also frequently cited as an icon by the gay community, something, he said, that flattered him – and there aren't many footballers who would be willing to say that. David, in fact, was becoming something extraordinary: not only a truly brilliant footballer, but a truly modern icon for our times. He wears make-up, he hardly even notices when people tease him about it, he cries unashamedly at events like his son's birth, he cooks, he treats Victoria superbly well and there aren't even any vices in the background like smoking and excessive drinking. If you were to make up all the ingredients for a role model for today, you would come up with David Beckham – and no one would believe that one man could be so perfect.

Also, he was a pretty good footballer. Cradling the Champions Cup after the Bayern Munich match, David yet again vowed his loyalty to the club, not least because he knew he was an increasingly attractive proposition to other European clubs. 'I always want to be a Manchester United player, of course I do,' he said exultantly. 'When you do things like winning the European Cup, why would you want anything else? Why go anywhere else? It couldn't possibly get better wherever I went.

'I'll play whatever position the manager wants me to. I have no problem with that – whether it's the centre or wide right. The enjoyable part of being a footballer is playing week in, week out, and that's all I can ask for. I have never wanted to be out of the side and I haven't felt in need of a rest. It's been a tough season of hard work, but when you end up with three trophies, as we have, you know all the hard work has been worth it. You can't better it, of course, but you can repeat it and this win gives us the incentive to go on and look to the future because we want to win all three again.'

It was practically a declaration of love to Manchester United. At that point, the great question was not whether Sir Alex would sell David, but whether Beckham would leave of his own accord. And David, a man of integrity, wanted to make it absolutely clear where his loyalties lay. The only problem – in Ferguson's eyes if in no one else's – was that he had another life, a very different life, in the south of England. And Sir Alex was beginning to think that perhaps the two would not mix.

But others were not so concerned. Kevin Keegan had briefly taken over as England coach from Glenn Hoddle after Hoddle sparked a row when airing his views on reincarnation, and Keegan was impressed. 'We've got a lot of captains in the side,' he said, 'and David has shown true leadership qualities recently. We all saw them against Bayern Munich.' It was a hint of more glories to come.

David was also beginning to realise that, against his own expectations, he was winning the public round. Girls fancied him, men admired him and children wanted to be him. It was quite a change from the previous year and David was loving every minute of it. 'I love having little kids look up to me and young players looking up to me and respecting me,' he crowed. 'That's something I always did as a youngster when I looked up to great players like Bryan Robson and Bobby Charlton. That's exactly how I want to be looked at. I don't want to be looked at with people saying horrible things about me off the pitch, either.'

David was also very sensible about his relationship with the media. The world of celebrity is filled with people who would sell their own grandmother to get their picture in the paper and then complain about the intrusion of privacy, but David was not one of them. He was straightforward and open about it and he didn't complain. Quite the opposite. 'At the moment, everything is perfect,' he said. 'That's a nice feeling to have. We've won the treble, I'm in the England squad, playing regularly – and, of course, my private life is perfect, too, with my new little boy.

'I think you do grow up when you have kids. People said that to me, but I've just started to realise it now. It's the best feeling in the world. I think if you go through an experience like I did after last summer you can either crack up or you can come out and make people eat their words. I feel that's what I have done. There were a lot of things said that I didn't care about, but it was worse for my mum and dad than it was for me. I don't get any privacy, only in my own home when the curtains are closed. Apart from that, that's it. There are so many people trying to get into my life and have a piece of me but I've come to learn to accept that. It's gone on for the whole year since the summer. But I've got on with it and grown up and I'm enjoying things.'

The euphoria couldn't last and there was, indeed, a blip: England drew 0–0 against Sweden, putting hopes of qualifying for the Euro 2000 finals on a knife edge. It didn't help that David pulled a hamstring and was thus unable to play in the next match. But everything else was going so well in his life that it hardly seemed to matter. The wedding was now less than a month away and David and Victoria were spotted carrying on business as usual: they were pictured going shopping in London's Knightsbridge – with David flashing the cash quite as much as his bride-to-be.

Beckham's parents were understandably delighted with all the praise and good fortune being heaped on their talented boy. Ted was asked if he'd felt let down by David's actions in the previous year's World Cup. 'No, not at all – it's only a game of football, after all – but I know that David felt he'd let his teammates down,' he said. 'After the game, we went up to him and cuddled him. I think he was upset for the older players, because he knew they wouldn't get another chance to play in the World Cup. Everybody was upset with David, but to slaughter a player like the press did is beyond me. More could have been done to protect him.'

Sandra went on to talk about what David was like as a little boy. 'He was a bit of an artist,' she said, 'always drawing cartoon characters. I've kept all his old sketchbooks. And he was very tidy and would make his own bed every day. Even now he can't stand mess. He was never naughty – except for the time he got his ear pierced when he was 14. He'd asked me if he could do it and I'd said no, because it could be dangerous if he'd got his earring caught on something when he was playing football. But he did it anyway. He came in the front door and ran straight upstairs, so I knew something was wrong. I let him keep the earring in, but he soon decided he didn't like it any more and stopped wearing it.' It was a telling comment – the only time David had been naughty in childhood was over a fashion statement.

Ted went on to recall the time when David first became interested in football. 'I've always been a big football fan and a Manchester United supporter,' he said. 'As a young man I played football for Leyton Orient and Walthamstow. I used to run a Sunday league side and David used to come with me from the age of four or five. When the game was over, he and I would practise on the pitch together, kicking and shooting till half-past ten or eleven o'clock at night. I knew he was good. He had things I'd never seen in a little kid before – he had crossing ability and control. He never said he wanted to be anything else other than a footballer, and he always said that one day he was going to play for Manchester United.'

David was clearly destined to be a footballer right from the outset. Sandra went on to reveal more about David's abilities when he was little more than a toddler. 'We used to take lots of cine-films when David was little and in every one he's got a ball,' she said. 'We've got a film of him at 18 months, wearing a little Manchester United strip. We've kept all his United kits since then. From the age of seven, he used to play in the park across the road, where I knew he'd be safe. I had a friend who worked in the hut there, and I used to ring and tell her he was on his way so she could keep an eye on him.'

It also went without saying that David's other great interest as a child had been fashion. 'He always dressed very well,' said Ted. 'Whenever he asked for clothes for his birthday, it had to be a designer name. He was always good-looking and always quite popular with girls. He never went through an ugly-duckling stage, although I remember him being quite self-conscious when he lost his teeth.'

'As a child, David was quite short for his age,' added Sandra. 'When he went to Manchester United at the age of 16, he was smaller than me. I'm five foot four.' 'He shot up the following year,' said Ted. 'They must've put him in a growbag! I remember going to see him in Manchester and talking to Nobby Stiles. He used to say to me, "Don't worry, Mr Beckham, he'll be six foot one day." And he was right!'

Perhaps unsurprisingly, David was not an academic little boy. 'He didn't do much reading,' Sandra admitted, 'but he'd read former Man United captain Bryan Robson's autobiography, in which Bryan said he drank a raw egg mixture to help him build his strength. So he did that for a while.'

Did David's parents worry about the amount of publicity the two were attracting? 'Yes, for their sake,' said Sandra. 'I think it is really sad that they cannot just go for a walk with the baby, like we used to do with David and the others when they were young. David and Victoria both came along to Ted's 50th birthday party last year. We told all the guests not to ask them for photographs or autographs and nobody bothered them at all. They were able to dance and enjoy themselves, just do those little things which ordinary couples are able to do, but which they can't.'

That was, of course, the downside of their fame. But there was an upside, too, and a big one at that. While accepting that there was much they couldn't do that normal couples wouldn't even think about, the fact is that the pair of them love being famous – hence the tour of the United States in the summer of 2003, an attempt to crack the last country in which they were not instantly recognisable. And the two of them adore what their fame brings: beautiful clothes, fabulous houses and a jewellery collection that by this time must match that of the Queen, to name but a few of fame's advantages. David and Victoria are highly media savvy and fully aware that the day the cameras, the press et al lose interest is the day that they turn back into ordinary human beings. And they don't want that – and are honest enough to admit it.

Very unusually for such a famous couple, David and Victoria had an extremely strong support system: each other. Quite apart from the desire to remain famous, the two have an enormous amount in common and a bond that has simply grown and deepened as the years go by. The cynics who dismiss their relationship as a carefully cultivated media image could not be more wrong: it is utterly genuine. The two have found in each other that for which we all hanker: their other half. In this world of celebrity break-up and divorce – to say nothing of marital breakdown for the rest of us – it is sometimes easy to forget that there are genuinely devoted couples, and David and Victoria are just that.

Writer Rebecca Cripps, who has spent time with the couple, bears that out. 'David and Victoria's secret is that they never take each other for granted and are tuned into each other's emotional needs,' she said. 'They spend so long apart that they really cherish the time they have together. David writes her adorable little notes saying, "I love you", which he hides under her pillow, slips into her dressing-gown pocket or tucks in drawers where she will find them. And she has driven hundreds of miles just to spend 30 minutes with him.'

The wedding was drawing near. More details began to leak out: there were to be 340 guests, all of whom had been asked to wear black so that the bride and groom could stand out in white. Geri had found that she had other arrangements: she would be playing at the annual fundraising concert Party In The Park that Sunday. Victoria would be leaving the word 'obey' out of the service. David had installed a new £15,000 shower in the couple's Cheshire home. All right, that wasn't strictly wedding-related but the public hunger for snippets about the glamorous couple was now so strong that even the most trivial of details were lapped up. There was also intense speculation as to where they would be spending the honeymoon, with hotels all over the country claiming the bride and groom would be sleeping there.

And, in true new-man style, David cancelled his stag night in order to spend a quiet evening in with Victoria. He had been due to hit the town with Gary and Phil Neville, Nicky Butt and Paul Scholes, but at the last minute decided to stay in with Victoria instead. 'He told them he wanted to spend as much time with Posh and Brooklyn before the wedding as possible,' said a friend. 'He feels it is his duty to be as supportive as possible at the moment. Posh is excited but also very nervous. And she needs as much reassurance from David as brides-to-be usually need from their fiancés. It's not that she can't be without him for the night – it's more that he didn't want to be without her.

'He is very aware of his responsibility towards her and Brooklyn. And, to be honest, he prefers to spend time with them more than anyone else. Brooklyn had that hernia operation a few weeks ago and he's teething now. So David felt he should put his role as a father first. Gary Neville is going to be his best man at the wedding anyway and Phil, Nicky and Paul will be there too. It's not like they minded. They are all great mates and understood entirely.'

In fact, the two could hardly bear to be away from each other at all. Victoria also had no plans for a hen night as she would rather have spent the time with David. 'She prefers to have a few close friends round to her home, cook a meal and have a laugh,' said the friend. 'That's what she will do instead of hitting the town. She and David are happiest when they are alone together. Even the idea of spending the night before the wedding apart isn't one they like. They'll both spend it with their parents, going through the final details. But no doubt they will get on the phone to each other.'

And, just temporarily at least, they enlisted the services of a nanny. They had hired Bentley's Entertainments to look after the wedding and the company was run by Peregrine Armstrong-Jones, half-brother of Lord Snowdon and his wife Caroline. 'I'm Posh Spice but you really are posh,' said Victoria brightly when they were introduced. They all got on so well together that the Armstrong-Joneses lent them their nanny to look after Brooklyn while preparations were ongoing.

The day before the wedding, the couple posed outside Victoria's parents' front door in Goff's Oak. David, dressed in black jeans and a white vest, said that he was calm and relaxed, adding, 'I'm not at all nervous.'

'I am a bit shaky but okay,' said Victoria who was wearing a leather miniskirt slit to the thigh, before bursting into a fit of giggles.

Photographer Humphrey Nemar was present. 'I have been taking snaps of Posh for years but I've never seen her look so happy and beautiful,' he said. 'She genuinely looked radiant. David looked over the moon. But then he should – he's about to get hitched to one of the world's most beautiful women who's also worth a few quid.'

Later that day the couple and their families flew to Dublin on a private jet as their guests also began to assemble in Ireland. En route to the airport they also got a surprise: Victoria's father Tony had phoned Radio 2 to request a special song for his daughter. He told DJ Ed Stewart that the pair of them would be tuning in to the show and asked him to play the Stevie Wonder song 'Sir Duke'.

A ring of steel had been set up outside the castle, which only intensified speculation as to what was going on inside. The reception, it was said, was going to be costing at least £500,000, although no one yet knew what it was really going to be like.

At last, the big day loomed. The guests, including Sir Bobby Charlton and David Seaman, began arriving at Dublin airport, from where they were taken to the castle itself. Assorted footballers and Spice Girls mingled with personal friends of the couple, with everyone in excellent spirits. It was noted that, of all the footballers present, many were carrying golf bags, while their wives and girlfriends attempted to outdo one another on the glamour front. The local villagers around the castle pretended they weren't unduly bothered by the assembly of stars gathered in their midst but were clearly as excited as everyone else by this marriage of the worlds of football and showbusiness. And, at long last, it was time for the wedding of the year: that of David Beckham to Victoria Adams.

CHAPTER 6

I TAKE THEE...

The sun dawned bright on 4 July 1999. Luttrellstown Castle had never looked more beautiful: it was a fairytale setting for what had been a fairytale romance. And now, finally, two years after they met, David Beckham and Victoria Adams were going to tie the knot.

Months of preparation had led up to the big day. Bentley Entertainments had been in charge of the planning, but the couple, especially Victoria, had also had a good deal of say. 'David and Victoria had a huge input right from the start,' said Peregrine Armstrong-Jones. 'The wedding has been 14 months in the planning, during which time the couple have been all over the world. Wherever they were, I would get samples, fabrics and plans to them and Victoria would often ring me fives times a day with ideas and questions.'

First, of course, they had had to find the right location.

'Victoria wanted somewhere really private and unique, somewhere green and leafy, deep in the countryside,' said Peregrine. 'Architecturally speaking, she didn't want anywhere too stuffy and she felt the castle had clean lines and grand proportions without being too imposing.' Once the locations had been chosen, David and Victoria then decided on a Robin Hood theme for the wedding, with lots of greenery, twigs, apples and fabric coloured burgundy, dark green and purple. They also had not one but two florists on hand: Simon Lycett, who did the flowers for *Four Weddings and a Funeral*, and John Plested, whose clients included the Queen.

The proceedings began at about three o'clock in the afternoon, as family members began to gather in the entrance hall of the castle. Fresh apples had been sewn into an ivy arrangement along the banisters, and the apples pierced to emit a sweet smell into the air. A leafy walkway led across the lawns to a huge marquee. 'I still can't believe it,' said Sandra Beckham, who was wearing a white Frank Usher suit. 'All the things we've talked about for months are actually here.'

Ted was equally bowled over. 'It's just something special – a fairytale,' he said. 'Victoria's an absolutely lovely girl and I feel very, very proud of the pair of them.' He was also enthusing about meeting Sir Bobby Charlton. 'He was my absolute hero when I was a youngster and my favourite moment was when I got to meet him alongside David. He was everything I'd imagined he would be – and a bit more.'

In fact, just about everyone was overwhelmed. 'When I

went into the marquee with Victoria earlier, the orchestra was rehearsing "Goodbye", a special version of the Spice Girls' Christmas hit and I got so emotional we had to have a bit of a cuddle,' said Victoria's father Tony. 'In fact, I got so emotional I had to take a bike out and cycle round the golf course to get over it! I didn't think I'd ever be emotional. I can be as hard as nails at times, but today – I mean this whole thing has been on the drawing board for so long and to see it coming together is very, very moving.'

By half-past three the bridesmaids – Victoria's sister Louise, her daughter Liberty and David's niece Georgina – appeared. The two little girls were dressed as woodland flower fairies, complete with wings and coronets, while Louise wore a dress by Chloé. It was a fitted cream corset decorated with copper and gold flowers and diamonds and a long cream skirt. All three bridesmaids had been given Tiffany diamond necklaces by the bride and groom. David's best man Gary Neville was given a Cartier watch while the usher, Victoria's brother Christian, received a Rolex. Finally, the rest of the Spice Girls arrived, plus Jimmy Gulzar and Phoenix Chi his daughter with Mel, and a fleet of Mercedes drew up in front of the castle to take the guests to the folly, where the marriage would actually take place. All the rest of the guests were only going to the reception.

The folly was a tiny chapel hanging above a stream, about 500 metres from the castle. 'The folly was a ruin and very cave-like when we found it, but Victoria loved the look of it,' said Peregrine. 'We had to do a lot of work to get it ready for the day – we had to bring builders in, put up scaffolding, lay a new floor and install power.'

The Bishop of Cork, the Right Reverend Paul Colton, was officiating at the ceremony. 'I don't see the ceremony as a marriage between two celebrities, but of a couple who are very much in love,' he said. 'They have had the same preparation and consultations as any other couple I have ever married.'

Victoria's dress, which she described as 'very Scarlett O'Hara', was in champagne-coloured satin, with a tight bodice and full skirt. Underneath it she wore a corset by Mr Pearl. Her shoes were also Vera Wang and on her head she wore a diamond and gold coronet by Slim Barrett. She was also wearing a beautiful diamond crucifix, which David had bought her for Christmas and which she had never worn before. David, meanwhile, was wearing a cream suit by Timothy Everett.

The couple had had rings designed by Asprey and Garrard. Victoria's was a marquise-set diamond supported on either side by three grain-set baguette diamonds and set in 18-carat yellow gold. David's was a full eternity ring, with 24 baguette diamonds and 24 smaller diamonds set in yellow gold. As a wedding present, David had given Victoria a pair of Asprey and Garrard emerald-cut diamond earrings set in 18-carat gold to match her ring, as well as a gold waist chain. Victoria gave him a Breguet watch.

Inside the folly itself, a string quartet had been entertaining the guests. But at 4.32 p.m., fashionably late, Victoria arrived on the arm of her father and waiting for her at the altar, with a sleeping Brooklyn in his arms, was David. Victoria walked up the aisle to the tune of Wagner's 'Bridal Chorus' from *Lohengrin* and the service began. 'They have chosen to be married according to the rites of the Church of Ireland and we are their supporters,' said the Bishop of Cork. David and Victoria smiled.

The reading, delivered by Reverend Lynda Peilow, was from John 15, 9–12: 'As the father has loved me, so I have loved you; abide in my love.' At this, David placed a kiss on Victoria's shoulder. After a short musical interlude, the Right Reverend Colton began his address. 'David and Victoria, Victoria and David, the marriage service doesn't give us a way of putting these names in order but, through your whole married life, you put each other first.' Everything about the service, every sight and sound was beautiful, he went on – 'except that', and gestured at a helicopter flying overhead.

But why do we do this, he asked. 'Why do we make everything so beautiful? It's simply because words fail us at a time like this. So we do all these beautiful things because they say better than words can: "Thank you" and "I love you". There is a lot of interest in this marriage and we are all excited to be here. But what matters is what is in David's heart and what is in Victoria's.'

The bishop warned against empty infatuation: 'The eyes that over cocktails seem so very sweet may not seem so amorous over Shredded Wheat,' which got a smile from Victoria. He then said that the key to a happy marriage was good communication, caring for people and 'finding a place for God and for spirituality in your lives'.

The couple were then called upon to face the congregation, where the banns were called. Since no one had any just cause or impediment to stop the wedding, he then put the couple's hands together before starting the marriage vows. At 4.49 p.m., the couple were pronounced man and wife. There was a whoop from the audience, cheers and clapping and a radiant David and Victoria kissed each other.

The newly married couple then knelt down at the altar and prayers were said: 'Almighty God, giver of life and love, bless Victoria and David, whom you have now joined in marriage. Grant them wisdom and devotion in their life together, that each may be to the other a strength in need, a comfort in sorrow and a companion in joy.' And then, just before 5 p.m., the couple walked up the aisle together to the tune of Mendelssohn's 'Wedding March'. Possibly the most famous couple in the world had been united in matrimony. 'It was very lovely,' said Victoria's sister Louise. 'I think everybody there was in tears.'

Back at the castle, the reception was getting under way. Guests were greeted by pageanters in Irish costume, while David and Victoria's crest flew on a flag above the castle. Inside was a 15-feet-tall floral arrangement, while guests were offered Laurent Perrier pink champagne, elderflower cordial with raspberries or Sicilian red orange juice. Canapés were also served before everyone made their way to the marquee. It had also been decorated in Robin Hood style: it was carpeted in deep red, while ivory taffeta adorned the sides. There were spectacular flower arrangements in burgundy, green and purple, and the tables were covered in dark green overlaid with cream linen calico and table decorations consisting of apples, candles and greenery. Moss-coloured candles were everywhere, and there were two huge chandeliers, also dressed in apples and greenery. 'It was a Robin Hood look meets Conran forest,' said Simon Lycett. David and Victoria themselves sat apart in their own private alcove, with Brooklyn in his favourite swinging chair at their side.

Dinner was a simple affair, as Victoria had already said she didn't want 'fiddled with' food. It consisted of tomato and red pepper soup, served in hollowed out pumpkins rather than bowls; chicken, asparagus, roast potatoes, French bean and sugar snap pea and herb jus; and then a choice of sticky toffee pudding with butterscotch (David's favourite) or summer berry terrine. In the background the 18-piece orchestra played a repertoire including the Spice Girls' hit 'Say You'll Be There' – the accompanying video to which afforded David his first sight of Victoria.

At 10.30 p.m. the couple cut the cake and speeches began. 'Ladies and gentlemen, many people would like to be here today but it is you that David and Victoria have chosen,' Tony Adams began. 'It is with great pride that I speak to you for a few moments about our bride and groom. Obviously, it is very difficult for me to find anything that hasn't already been written by the *News Of The World*, the *Sun*, the *Daily Mirror* – need I go on?'

Victoria, he continued, had never been any trouble. 'She started dance classes at the age of three and was soon rushing home from school to change from her uniform into a leotard to kick her legs about – little did she know that, only a few miles away, there was a little boy changing from his uniform into shorts to kick a ball around. They continued with enthusiasm and at 16 both left home to continue their training. Victoria went to dance college in Epsom and we all know where David went. As it happened, they both did quite well.'

Tony went on to describe how David saw Victoria on video and how the two finally met, before ending, 'This afternoon I have given David someone who is very precious to me, but I know he will look after her, as he always does, with the utmost love and affection. We know we couldn't wish for a better son-in-law.' He asked guests to stand and wish 'our bride and groom a life of love and happiness – to the rest of the world they are Posh and Becks, but to us they are David and Victoria'.

Now it was David's turn. 'Thank you, Tony, for that speech – that meant more to us than you'll ever know,' he began. 'My wife and I' – that brought the ceiling down – 'would like to thank you for coming. I'm sure you'll agree that all the bridesmaids looked absolutely beautiful and stunning and I'd like to say that our mums have scrubbed up very well today, too! No, seriously, they look stunning.

'What can I say? My mother- and father-in-law have loved and supported me and been there for me and obviously that means the world to me. Jackie and Tony have given me something very precious to them. I will love and look after Victoria and treat her like a princess – which she always wants to be treated like.'

Turning to Victoria's brother, he continued, 'Christian, I've always wanted a brother and that's how I feel about you. And I feel just as close to Louise. I'd also like to thank my mum and dad who have brought me up from a young age – obviously! – and my sisters, who have been there from day one – obviously! Also, my nan and granddad who, in a few weeks, will be celebrating their 50th anniversary – I love you!'

And then it was a tribute to the best man. 'If Gary Neville's performances have been a bit shaky in the last few months, now you know why,' said David. 'He's been disappearing off to the toilet, wiping his brow and looking very worried. But Gary has always been there for me when I've needed him – especially when Victoria was away and I needed someone to talk to. I'd like to say that I really love you, Gary, and you'll notice we kiss a lot on the pitch!'

Finally, David turned to the most important people of all. 'This has been a massive year for us but she couldn't have given me a better present than the one she presented me with four months ago,' he said. 'I think "love" is a very strong word and all my love goes to Victoria and Brooklyn. Victoria wakes up every day and she seems to get more beautiful every time I see her. I know a lot of people say we've done it the wrong way around – had Brooklyn and then got married – but if you've got love, nothing else matters.'

And so, finally, to Gary Neville. 'He speaks well, that Julian Clary, doesn't he?' he began. Gary first thanked the bishop and everyone at the castle, then gave his apologies to the Spice Girls for the fact that Bayern Munich were not in attendance before saying he had a telegram from Diego Simeone – at which he held up a red card. Then there was a real telegram from Sir Alex Ferguson, who was attending another wedding elsewhere, various other messages of goodwill and finally something, 'from Prada, Gucci, Tiffany, British Telecom and Ferrari – best wishes and thanks for your support'.

Gary then talked about his friendship with David. 'David's outgoing and bubbly – I'm a bit of a moaning, miserable git,' he said. 'People are always asking me why I always kiss David Beckham. My answer is that I'd usually do much more than that to a six-foot blond in shorts with legs up to the armpits!' As for David's feelings about Victoria – 'He would come into training every day like a little schoolboy – you'd go a long way to find two people more madly in love.'

Finally, he turned to Victoria and told her she looked beautiful, before finishing, 'Brooklyn and Victoria have made David the happiest person in the world and that, in turn, has made me happy and everyone else in the room. Ladies and gentlemen – enjoy the evening and drink away!'

Everyone took him at his word. After dinner, the guests were led into a second marquee, which was decorated in Moroccan style, with luxurious gold and purple drapes and huge gold statues bearing flowers. The dance floor was painted in a black-and-white chequerboard design and surrounded by chaises longues and huge velvet and leopard-skin cushions with low-level tables.

David and Victoria slipped away and changed into their second outfits of the evening in matching purple designed by Antonio Berardi. Victoria's dress was what she termed a 'Jessica Rabbit' dress – a clinging, strapless gown of purple stretch satin, split to the thigh with a bright red lining. David was wearing a matching purple suit and had his hair up in a quiff – and even Brooklyn wore purple. The evening ended in riotous fun as the assembled footballers, Spice Girls and friends partied with a vengeance. The night was a triumph.

The whole affair was covered by *OK! Magazine* for £1 million and the two gave a lengthy interview afterwards. They first talked about choosing the venue. 'We spent a lot of time in Ireland when Victoria started her tour in Dublin and we felt at home here,' said David. 'The people are lovely – the photographers even asked our permission before they took a picture and, if we said. "No", they walked away.'

They were asked why they chose to marry in the folly. 'There isn't a church on the estate, so we had to find a location on the premises we could get licensed for a wedding ceremony,' said Victoria. 'We were just driving and we found the folly, which was in a complete state – a hermit had been living there. It was overgrown, half the floor was missing and there were big holes in the walls – it was like walking into a garden shed. But we just looked at each other and said, "This is the place." It was just big enough for our closest family and friends. I wanted the ceremony to be as private as possible.'

They were then asked if the celebrations were over the top. 'Whatever we do, we know we're going to get criticised,' said Victoria. 'Some people will say it's over the top. But then, if we'd had a small wedding, they would have said, "Couldn't they have done something bigger?" A lot of stuff is tongue-in-cheek. For example, we've got a flag on top of the castle with our initials, VDB, on it. We don't care what people say – as long as we're happy and our families are happy, that's all that matters.'

And why did David pick Gary Neville as his best man? 'Gary's been my closest friend since I moved to Manchester,' he said. 'I'm close to the whole team, but Gary's always been there when I've needed to talk to someone. We're the best of friends – I'm always round at his house. He was really pleased when I asked him to be best man. I know he's been very nervous about making his speech but he's a very good speaker at functions and I knew he'd be wicked.'

For a couple who were so often accused of flashiness, David and Victoria made an inspired choice when it came to wedding presents: they asked guests for vouchers for Marks & Spencer or Selfridges or suggested they made a donation to the Meningitis Trust. And would their relationship change once they were married? 'No, not at all,' said David. 'We've been a really close couple since day one. Obviously, Brooklyn's arrival has brought us closer together, definitely. There's three of us now and there's a lovely family atmosphere at home. Nothing could make us any closer than we already are.'

And so the wedding of the year, if not the decade, ground to a close. David was clearly blissfully happy: as a mature individual, being a family man clearly suited him. And he had married very well. Whatever the reservations of Sir Alex Ferguson and assorted others, Victoria was absolutely the right woman for him. Apart from the fact that they were and are absolutely besotted with one another, their union was to make the two of them one of the most famous couples on the planet. As individuals they had already made their mark but together they really were greater than the sum of their two parts. Victoria was already becoming more famous for her relationship with David than as a Spice Girl and as for David – his profile was to become so great that it actually overshadowed one of the most famous football clubs in the world.

But that was still to come. In the heady days after the marriage, the couple flew off to the South of France for a brief honeymoon to revel in being married and to calm down after all the excitement.

Back in Britain, however, there were rumblings of

discontent from David's side of the family. Right from the start, the Beckhams had seen David becoming close to Victoria's family – indeed, he mentioned them before his parents in his bridegroom's speech – and now his great-uncle Peter, the brother of his grandfather, had his say. 'We hardly ever see David these days,' he said. 'It's such a shame. We used to be really close, but we have just drifted apart. He has changed since he met Victoria. That is what women do to men, isn't it?'

David and Victoria were learning the hard way that weddings could be as divisive among families as open warfare.

Warming to his theme, Peter, an electrician, continued, 'Don't get me wrong – Victoria is a lovely girl, generous almost to a fault and very shy, like David. But she's not necessarily the girl I'd have picked for my son. I'm not sure why things turned out the way they did. I think it's because the families are worlds apart. I've met Victoria's family. They think the world of David but we don't get on as well.'

The problem, it seemed, boiled down to class. Although Posh wasn't quite as posh as everyone initially thought, it was true that the Adams family had money and the Beckhams didn't. That was the root of the problem. 'Yet the Adams family are no different from anybody else except they've got a few bob extra,' said Peter. 'At the end of the day, they are just ordinary people with a famous daughter, like the Beckhams are ordinary people with a famous son.'

Peter had not been invited to the wedding. 'I was so

disappointed – I've always understood weddings are for families,' he said. 'But the only people invited were David's parents, his sister, her fiancé and one uncle. Don't ask me why. Yet there were celebrities there with girlfriends they had only just met. I think it's wrong. Mind you, when I read about it, I wasn't quite as disappointed. That lavish display didn't fit in with what I know of David. It was rather extravagant and over the top – the word "tacky" springs to mind. But I think that's probably Victoria's influence, not David's.

'We've only seen his son Brooklyn once and that was accidental – we bumped into them in Marks and Spencers. We are disappointed we haven't seen more of him. I don't know why we haven't, although work obviously comes into it. Also, David's got a new life now. He's still extremely close to his parents, though.'

It was a harsh statement coming from a member of the family – and one who clearly felt left out. But what Peter failed to understand was that, in many ways, David and Victoria now needed only one another. Although they were close to their parents, their world was complete, especially now they had a child to bind them together. Friends of the couple speak of the fact that, when they're together, they are so absorbed in one another that they almost seem cut off from the world outside.

But the world outside continued to exist and it wasn't only David's family who had something to say about the wedding. The couple had hoped to honeymoon on an island in the Indian Ocean but had to opt for France instead when Sir Alex

Ferguson refused to allow David to take off three days extra. The message was clear: it's fine to get married, but never forget that football comes first.

As autumn rolled on, the couple's profile continued to soar. They were interviewed for the September edition of *Vanity Fair* and appeared on the cover; the interview was notable not only for the sensuous pictures of the two of them rolling all over one another, but also for Victoria's defence of her husband's intellect. 'He's actually a really intelligent person,' she said. 'He's really deep, which I like. He's really frustrated because people think that, because he doesn't say a lot, he doesn't have a brain.' She went on to joke, 'We played Trivial Pursuit the other day and I was devastated – I got beaten by David Beckham!'

Victoria is spot-on about her husband's intelligence. Because David has, to put it bluntly, a silly voice, it's easy to credit him with less nous than he has. But, if you look at the evidence, you see a hugely rich man with a happy marriage, international profile and the maturity to cope with pressures that have all but destroyed the likes of Paul Gascoigne and George Best. David may not be a great intellectual but he possesses a wisdom denied not only to fellow footballers but most of the rest of us.

It is this wisdom that makes him such a likeable fellow and it also means he is totally unconcerned about matters that make other football stars go hot under the collar. That same autumn he was picked as part of an ideal gay team by the magazine

Attitude for having 'the face of an angel and the bum of a Greek god'. David laughed it off. Even he, however, had his sang-froid tested in a match against Leeds at Old Trafford, making a V sign at the rival fans. For once, public opinion was completely behind him and he was not penalised: the fans had been jeering and making truly disgusting comments about Victoria and Brooklyn. A man's patience could only be tested so far.

And finally, after months of speculation, the couple bought what was to be their main home. Set in 24 acres of grounds, with an indoor swimming pool, the £2.5-million house was immediately and inevitably dubbed Beckingham Palace. The grounds contained ponds and an ornamental fountain; inside, the entrance hall contained an oak staircase and a magnificent chandelier. There was a huge dining room leading to the pool, an immaculate kitchen, breakfast room and study, along with seven bedrooms and an attached two-bedroom cottage. It was perfect and, even better, it was in Sawbridgeworth on the Hertfordshire – Essex border – close to both Victoria's parents and Stansted airport.

To celebrate, David bought a new car to add to his collection – a £92,000 Aston Martin DB7 to go with his Ferrari and Range Rover. He and Victoria also hit the town, prompting the usual concerns that his showbiz lifestyle would affect his football, not least when he appeared at a London party to launch Jade Jagger's jewellery collection less than 12 hours before he was due to fly out of Manchester with United to Austria.

Sir Alex was asked for his opinion and contented himself with a 'No comment'. However, his autobiography, *Managing My Life*, had recently been published, and in that he was more open about his feelings about Beckham. 'There was a period when I was troubled by the amount of travelling he was doing in his private life and about whether he was getting enough rest,' he wrote. 'Two or three trips a week to Ireland to be with Victoria was not an ideal preparation for what was being asked of him on the park and I had to stress that he had obligations to his own talent and his teammates. Fortunately, that is no longer a concern. Now Victoria and David have settled in Cheshire with their baby son Brooklyn, normal habits have been resumed.'

That was an extremely rare case of wishful thinking on Sir Alex's part. The couple had not fully settled in Cheshire – their main home was 200 miles away. And Victoria later admitted that she had been known to suggest to David that she'd be happier if he moved to a club down south. But at the time, everyone was keen to make and keep the peace – to a certain extent. It later emerged that the club fined David £50,000 as a penalty for his unauthorised night out – and, ironically enough, it was David's fashion sense that had given the game away. He attracted even more notice than usual because he was wearing a bandanna on his head – and so attracted Sir Alex's notice by appearing in all the papers.

But David let nothing come in the way of being a family man. He began to take Brooklyn to training – and, according to

Victoria, he would even make her a packed lunch before setting off for the day. The couple also got rid of their Rottweilers, according to some reports, fearing that the dogs might become jealous of Brooklyn. Brooklyn was indeed causing the couple some concern: in December, Victoria lunged at a man who seemed to be making threatening gestures as she and David left Harrods – David, of course, was holding the baby.

And Victoria continued to make controversial comments about her husband. As the year drew to an end, she accused United of underpaying him, pointing out that United captain Roy Keane was earning £50,000 – twice as much as David. Asked if she'd told him to approach Sir Alex, she replied, 'Certainly! Wouldn't you? I would love to say no but that would be lying.' Pouring oil on the flames, she continued that she wanted him to move abroad. 'I don't want to sound too shallow, but it's got to be somewhere a bit hot,' she continued. 'I don't want anywhere too grim. Italy, Spain, somewhere like that, I imagine. I think sometime in the future David would want to go abroad.'

She was right. But that time was still some way ahead. For now, David was quite simply a national hero.

CHAPTER 7

MILLENNIUM MAN

By the start of the new millennium, David's fame had grown so great that he was now the subject of security scares. United were due to fly to Brazil in early January to play in the World Club Championships and there were real fears that they might be the subject of a kidnapping attempt. In total, the club's players were worth at least £100 million, with David alone accounting for £30 million of that. The Brazilians were ordered to step up security. 'We have done everything we can to minimise the risk to the team,' said Rio police chief Major Marinho. 'We don't expect problems, but there is always the possibility of one.'

The team headed for Rio, with an anxious Victoria telling David to be careful. She had also repeated her comment in an interview to the effect that David wore her underpants, resulting in a further flurry of newspaper headlines. David had other things to worry about: in the opening game of the World Club Championship in Rio he was sent off during the team's first game against the Mexican side Necaxa. Fergie – who had also been told to leave the 'technical area' following a row with a FIFA official – was supportive. 'The Mexican players got David sent off,' he said, while dismissing his own contretemps – and the match ended in a 1–1 draw.

All of that was completely overshadowed when a Sunday newspaper ran a story claiming that there was indeed a kidnap plot – but it involved Victoria and Brooklyn, not David. Although it later turned out that the paper had paid £10,000 for a story without much foundation, it caused serious alarm, and the couple immediately arranged for increased security at all times.

The circus surrounding the family just continued to grow. Kevin Keegan, the then England manager, attempted to defuse some of the pressure when he said, 'To me, David Beckham is not a celebrity but a tremendously talented player – and that's all I'm interested in. In the back of my mind I know there are other things that come with him, with Michael Owen and with Alan Shearer. But they're not celebrities when they're with England. The problem people like David face is that everybody is trying to get a piece of the action because the media is a monster, which needs feeding constantly.

'But I've never seen any indication that the pressure is getting to David. He mixes well with all the boys. Whenever he comes in to the England squad he's a model player, and

I've never had any problems with him. He's a winner and it goes without saying he's a tremendous player. The judgement on David now, though, is either a positive or a negative – there's nothing in between. He's either at the top of the sky or down in the pits, but as a manager I try to go along a middle line.'

United were certainly only too keen to hang on to David at that time. His pay was inching ever higher, now at around the £60,000-a-week mark as the club sought to fend off interested rivals. And it was David's father, of all people, who hinted that, if the couple continued to be on the receiving end of unkind treatment, then they might pack up and go abroad. 'What has been going on is an absolute disgrace,' he said. 'I know how high profile David is, but there is more serious news going on than my lad being splashed all over the front pages. I think it is a shame because he's just a footballer, after all, and the media are trying to make him into something he isn't. He won't want to leave England but anything is possible at the end of the day.' When the day finally came, of course, it was not the media who pushed David abroad. But at that stage no one dreamed of the rift that was to develop between David and Sir Alex.

David responded to this in typical fashion: he put on his bandanna and went out to face the photographers. Victoria, meanwhile, went on TV chat show *Parkinson*, where she tackled the ongoing speculation as to whether David wore her knickers or not. 'It was a joke. I mean, as if he'd wear my knickers, come on,' she said.

But the damage was done. It had just given rivals fans yet another stick with which to beat poor Becks.

They certainly couldn't taunt him with his performance on the field, though. At the end of January, United beat Middlesborough 1–0, with David scoring a goal in the 88th minute, his first of the Premiership season. Football commentators were forecasting that his game could only get better: it was a much-needed boost after the public-relations fiasco in Rio.

And still his profile continued to rise. It seemed that hardly a day could go by without David making the news and, indeed, the latest news about the boy was that he now had a stalker. She'd taken to visiting the couple's Cheshire home and leaving love letters and gifts – including her knickers. The letters included one saying, 'Sex is strong – so believe in it!' Another read, 'Situation 69 is blowing my mind!'

This was not long after the kidnap threat to Victoria, and Beckham took no chances: he contacted the police. They, in turn, discovered that his stalker was a 14-stone, 36-year-old former escort girl called Chinyelu Obue. She, in turn, seemed a little bewildered by the fuss. 'I now know I've got no chance with him,' she said, after being warned off by the police. I'm usually 13 to 14 stone. I suppose that's a little different from what he's used to with Victoria. I've got my own sex appeal and plenty of admirers, but I admit I once wanted to sleep with David. Some stuff I wrote was a bit porno. I never wanted to hurt him. I just wanted to make him smile.'

He needed a smile. Given the intensification of media interest since his marriage to Victoria, David was again under the eagle eye of Sir Alex, and Sir Alex didn't like what he saw. The two were involved in a furious row during training in February, when the United manager accused David of spending time in London the previous day when he should have been training. The row got so intense that David finally threw his gloves away and stormed off United's new training ground in Carrington. He was later seen driving away in his black Range Rover, again fuelling speculation that he might be prepared to leave the club.

And, indeed, the situation promptly got worse. It emerged that David's absence had been caused by a health scare involving Brooklyn. The 11-month-old boy became ill during the night, prompting Victoria to phone a doctor at 3am. The doctor diagnosed gastro-enteritis. Wanting to stay home and care for his son, David phoned in to say he couldn't make training. 'Brooklyn was coughing and being sick in the middle of the night, and they called the doctor because they didn't know what was wrong with him,' said a spokesman for the couple. 'They were very worried. Obviously David wanted to stay with his son.'

But it was not obvious to Sir Alex. In his eyes this was not the way a footballer should behave and the sin was compounded by the fact that David was in Hertfordshire, not Cheshire. One row was nowhere near enough to clear the air: David was dropped from the forthcoming match against Leeds United and, not even picked for the substitutes' bench, was forced to watch the match from the stands.

'I picked the team for today and that's it,' said Sir Alex. 'In this situation I didn't pick David. What happened is just one of those things. What we do is inside the club and all things will be dealt with by the club.'

It didn't help that Victoria had been photographed at the British Fashion Awards ceremony on the night that David missed training, albeit without her spouse in tow. But it was the first really serious clash between player and manager since the wedding and many took it to be a sign of the increasing hold Victoria had over her husband. It was also the start of real tensions between the formidable Victoria and Sir Alex. The latter had never much cared for Victoria's world but now they had entered into a battle with one another for David's heart and soul and, right from the start, it was obvious who was going to win – Victoria. But when that finally happened, David would have to go.

Kevin Keegan stepped in to play peacemaker. He picked David to play midfield against Argentina – and no one missed the significance of that – when England played in a friendly. 'What happened at Leeds is a Manchester United thing and only two people can sort that out,' he said. 'It saddens Alex Ferguson, it saddens David Beckham and it saddens me. But sometimes manager and players have fallouts and you have to be realistic about that. But as far as I am concerned, David is fit and raring to go, as enthusiastic as ever, and was the last one off the training field as usual.

'On Wednesday, David can again show people what he can

do with a football. He might benefit from the chance to return from this setback in style because he has an awful lot going for him as a player and a person. I know some people have concerns but I am not worried about his temperament and I never have been. He will be champing at the bit to play and will find a way of doing the job I ask of him as he always does.

'I put my trust in him because to me he's just a footballer. People talk about the other things going on in his life and they underestimate him because they don't know him. People pick up the bits and build an image, which I don't think is the guy. Having talked with him, trained with him, worked with him, I don't share those opinions. I see a very determined character who loves playing football and those are the qualities you need at the top. I would not give him responsibility if I didn't think he had the talent or the temperament to handle it. This match will be the sort of challenge he will relish.' And indeed he did. The game ended in a 0–0 draw, but Beckham put in a good performance and for now, at least, the ructions died down.

David's love of his high-profile lifestyle, however, continued to grow. He and Victoria did a photo session with Annie Leibovitz, one of the world's top photographers, to be published in *Vanity Fair*. The two were pictured rolling around each other at the Cawdor Estates, Inverness, ending with a shot of Victoria straddling her husband as he lay on a pool table. The pictures were stunning – and did nothing to stop David's growing celebrity.

Nor did the couple hold back when it came to Brooklyn's

first birthday party. They laid on a £10,000 bash at Cotton's Hotel in Knutsford, Cheshire, inviting 100 guests along for the party. The theme was a circus, with no less than four clowns in attendance to amuse the assembled crowd. The children got burgers and the adults munched on lobster as little Brooklyn, dressed in a maroon bomber jacket with cream leather sleeves, held court. Guests included Gary Neville, with brother Phil and his wife Julie, Paul Scholes with wife and baby, Denis Irwin plus his three children and many more. Some adults, including Ryan Giggs and Mark Bosnich, turned up later. It was a resounding success.

'We have got him lots of toys,' said Victoria on her way in. 'It all looks fantastic in there.'

'It was a massive production,' said a member of the hotel's staff. 'Just converting the room at the back of the hotel into the way they wanted it took quite some time and plenty of effort. But there was plenty of laughter coming from the room. Brooklyn's parents really pushed the boat out and everyone obviously enjoyed the party.'

It also marked the end of the row between David and Sir Alex – for now, at least. David spoke publicly about the spat. 'It disappoints me that a little argument between me and the manager was blown up out of all proportion,' he said. 'I felt I had a good reason to miss training. Brooklyn was ill with gastro-enteritis. I rang the club and told them that. In the end I abided by what the manager and the club decided and accepted their disciplinary action. I have heard it said I'm trying to be bigger than the club. I'm not and never could be. Nobody can be bigger than the biggest club in the world.

'My relationship with the manager is fine. Players sometimes have bust-ups with their managers but it doesn't mean they have to fall out permanently. With our manager, you can have an argument with him one day and it will be forgotten the next. He's had his say and I've had mine. He's never mentioned it to me since and he doesn't bear grudges.'

Ferguson confirmed that it was all in the past. 'The players know I don't hold grudges,' he said. 'I haven't got the time to hold a grudge. I just want to get on with the game. That applies to all the players and David is no different from anyone else. I have had a chat with David. All we can say about him now is that the matter is cleared. It's over. It was finished on the day it began. I hope David is now saying the same positive things about the situation.'

He certainly was. Keen to ensure his loyalty to the club and smooth over any tensions between his wife and his manager, David could scarcely have been more positive. 'I love Manchester United with a passion,' he said. 'It's the only club I ever wanted to play for and I still do. Victoria doesn't want anything to affect that. She has never had a fallout with the manager. She respects him. People are trying to create a rift between them, but I can tell you, it doesn't exist.'

If that were not enough, David went on to talk about Victoria's feelings about Manchester. 'It's annoying that so many people seem to believe that Victoria hates Manchester and living up here,' he said. 'She spends much of her time in Manchester. The only time she's in London is when she's working. People seem to have this idea that I commute to work between London and Manchester every day. It's nonsense. We have an apartment in Alderley Edge and that is our home. It's where Victoria, Brooklyn and I live. We've bought a house down south and we'll probably live there eventually because that's where we both come from. But that is way in the future.' The message could not have been clearer. Everything in the garden was rosy and David had absolutely no intention of leaving Man U.

Despite the sudden outbreak of peace, though, David had no intention of adopting a lower profile. And so it was that startled fans saw a sharply crew-cut David run out on to the pitch when United played Leicester, having spent £300 having his locks trimmed. Any bemusement Sir Alex might have felt – and he almost certainly did – would have been allayed by the outcome of the match at least: United won 2–0, with one of the goals scored by Beckham. To celebrate, Brooklyn was given a similar cut.

Trivial as it was, David's haircut made both the front pages and the comment pages of the papers, with speculation rife about why he'd done it – to look more manly, said some, who clearly knew nothing about David's blithe disregard for his detractors – and whether he would lose his Brylcreem sponsorship. It was extraordinary that a man, and a footballer, to boot, should attract such attention merely over his appearance, but the public simply could not get enough of Posh and Becks. Every move the two of them made was reported on and every time they changed their partings there was saturation coverage. There was also a rumour that someone had been combing through the hair salon's rubbish bins to get their hands on David's shorn locks.

It is often asked why the two have such an appeal but the answer is simple: they are young, beautiful, rich and in love. They are Prince Charles and Princess Diana, except with a happy ending. They have a lifestyle that most people can only dream about and on top of that their devotion to one another is genuine. Who wouldn't want to be Posh or Becks? Who wouldn't want to look that good themselves, have that good-looking a spouse, have such a successful career and to be fêted wherever they went? It's no surprise David and Victoria enjoy their lifestyle – who wouldn't?

Of course, the one worry was Brooklyn and David acknowledged that. 'Fatherhood has changed me,' he said. 'I look at life from a different perspective. It's the best feeling and has made the relationship between me and Victoria even stronger. We'd like three or four kids but not yet. We want to enjoy watching Brooklyn grow up. We get worried for him because of all the attention we attract, which is why we have security with us at all times. But we try to act as normal as possible. We're doing our best.'

He was also keen to deny rumours to the effect that Victoria dominated him. 'She's always being asked who wears the trousers in the relationship,' he said. 'I can assure you, I'm my own man, but we make the big decisions about our life together. What some people don't realise is that Victoria says a lot of things tongue-in-cheek. The comment about me wearing her knickers was a joke. Everyone should have known that. But for four or five days it was all people wanted to talk about. It was embarrassing and she shouldn't have said it – even in jest. But then we had a laugh about it. It didn't cause any problems between us.'

David was also feeling sensitive about his reputation as a party animal. 'All people want to talk about is this person who wears sarongs and bandannas,' he grumbled. 'That annoys me. It seems to have been forgotten that I've spent most of my life working hard to earn a place in one of the top sides in the world. Some people are trying to turn me into a bad boy, which I never have been and never will be. I've never been pictured with a beer in my hand staggering all over the place. Occasionally we go to eat out at The Ivy, where you find a lot of celebrities. But we don't go there to be flash. When we visit some places we can't eat because people are coming up continually to ask for autographs. In The Ivy they don't let anyone ask for autographs. I know this because Michael Jordan was in there one night and I wasn't able to get his signature!'

David was, indeed, working hard, as were the rest of the team. United continued to go from strength to strength, receiving the Premier League Trophy in May. David shaved his head especially for the occasion and took Brooklyn on to the pitch. Roy Keane and Raymond van der Gouw also brought their own offspring on to the field, while Sir Alex cradled his grandson Jake.

As summer approached, David got his next tattoo: a figure of an angel looking down on the Brooklyn tattoo. Then a group of fans went one step further and decided that Beckham, too, should be a figure of worship. The fans, who lived in Thailand, made a 12-inch-high, gold-leafed statue of Becks, which they placed in the inner sanctum of the Pariwas temple in Bangkok. The monks didn't seem to mind. 'If it brings people to the temple, it will have done some good,' said one.

With Euro 2000 on the cards, attention finally turned back to the football field and playing for England. Kevin Keegan again voiced his support for the young star. 'Beckham can have a bigger influence on the England set-up than he has had already,' he said. 'I'm not scared to tell him because he knows that as well. There is no limit to how good he can become. He is still young, yet very experienced. Whatever he wants to be, he can be. There's so much more in him.'

Keegan was not alone in that opinion. Brazil ace Roberto Carlos told his teammates that the best way to ensure a victory is this: stop Beckham. 'Beckham is England's main player,' he said. 'Every time they have the ball, they look to get it to him. If he gets time and space to cross he will cause any team in the world problems.' There can be no higher praise than words such as this from a man you are to meet on the pitch. He was even voted second-best footballer in the world after Rivaldo.

David and Victoria took a short break in the States with Brooklyn before David reappeared, looking refreshed and ready for the trials ahead. Everyone was forecasting that he could be the best footballer in the world and now he seemed determined to make it happen. 'I've never felt better in my life,' he said. 'I've got bags of confidence right now. I've come off a good season, won another trophy and I've started to score goals. Now I want to dominate games for England more than I do. I really feel ready.'

And so Euro 2000 kicked off, with England playing Ukraine. Much to David's dismay, however, he again had to put up with abuse from the fans – many of them England fans who had still not forgotten the match against Argentina in 1998. David made a public plea for them to stop hating him and stand behind him, prompting words of comfort from a surprising quarter – Rivaldo.

'I have always had big pressure on me, it's nothing new – but since I was declared the best player there are new pressures,' he said. 'Although I know there are always people looking at what I do and how I play, I'm very calm and serene and try to do my job on the field. I keep working as hard as I've always done and I don't give too much significance to the pressure. When the game starts, I forget everything people tell me, everything people say about me, all the advice that newspapers or TV give me. I try to play my game with tranquillity and I think I am successful in doing that.

'That's the best way for Beckham to deal with things, just

switch off. I believe this is the way to cope with pressures. Each player has different ways of coping with it and I don't know what his personality is. And, in Beckham's case, there are different matters that may affect his performance because he has a very famous wife. People see him in a different light because of that and the pressure goes beyond the football pitch. But I can't really give him any advice because he knows what to do on the field and he should know his ways of handling it.'

Euro 2000 did not start well for England. The team lost 3–2 to Portugal, although David himself played brilliantly. When he went to acknowledge the fans, however, he received such a volley of abuse that he ended up giving them a one-fingered gesture. As with Leeds, no one blamed him. The fans concerned were a disgrace to their country and the match: they chanted threats against Brooklyn, before turning their putrid little minds to Victoria and calling her a whore.

Kevin Keegan was staunchly supportive. 'I'd have thumped them,' he declared angrily. 'It was the worst thing I've seen in football. I've taken plenty of abuse in my time but this was way beyond anything I've heard. It was very personal. If you'd heard that abuse, if your sons and daughters had to listen to that, you'd have reacted in the same way.'

The entire nation felt the way Keegan did and rallied to David's defence. David responded brilliantly and went on the attack: the second game went far better, with England beating Germany 1–0. This time round he walked off the field to cheering, partly in recompense for treatment he had received previously. And when, a few days later, England lost 3–2 to Romania and crashed out of Euro 2000, David, in particular, was given thunderous applause as he left the field.

It was a momentous occasion in more ways than one because, for the first time, speculation began to mount that David might captain England. Alan Shearer was retiring and, although Keegan had been talking of Tony Adams as his replacement, Adams had not played as well as Beckham in the previous matches and was no longer considered a sure thing.

Shearer himself called on Keegan to hand David the prize. 'I have a great deal of pride when I pull on an England shirt but to captain my country would be the ultimate dream for me,' said Beckham. 'I have always harboured dreams of captaining the teams I play for, be they Manchester United or England, and I can think of no greater honour.'

The weeks after Euro 2000 gave David some time with his family. Victoria was working hard to promote her first solo single, a collaboration with True Steppers and Dane Bowers called 'Out Of Your Mind', and David dutifully accompanied her on a series of appearances, including an appearance at Party In The Park. Loyal as ever, he stood in the front of the crowd videoing her – she was later criticised for miming – before giving her a big hug when she came off the stage. The couple proceeded to tour England to publicise the record, including a much-discussed appearance at Woolworth's in Oldham. David came in for criticism for trooping around after

Victoria and Victoria came in for criticism for dragging him around after her but, as ever, the couple blithely ignored the sniping and got on with their jobs.

But, while David might have been taking a rest from football, football was not taking a rest from him. Despite England's overall performance in Euro 2000, he had emerged with credit and was again being wooed by various rival clubs. This time around AC Milan had him in their sights and had approached Sir Alex to ask if he was for sale: the answer was no. At that time Sir Alex wouldn't hear of it and his decision was final.

David, Victoria and Brooklyn headed off for a quick break in the South of France, where they stayed first in the St Tropez villa of Harrods owner Mohamed Al Fayed and then at Sir Elton John's place near Nice. During their time at St Tropez, the couple were invited on to Fayed's yacht *Sakara*. 'David and Victoria looked really pleased to be invited on board,' said a friend. 'They were spotted joking and laughing with Mr Al Fayed as they all downed champagne in the sun. Posh and Becks got to know Mr Al Fayed through their frequent trips to his Harrods store. He had told them that his villa was always available if they wanted it.'

But then, to everyone's surprise, Sir Alex risked reopening old wounds on the publication of an updated version of his autobiography. He had written about the furious argument he'd had with David earlier in the year, which led to him dropping Beckham for the match with Leeds. 'It doesn't matter to me how high a player's profile is,' he wrote. 'If he is in the wrong, he is disciplined. And David was definitely in the wrong.' It emerged he was particularly angry that Victoria had ventured out while David stayed at home. 'I had to think that David wasn't being fair to his teammates,' he went on. 'I had to imagine how they would feel if David could adjust the schedule to suit himself. There was no way I could consider including Beckham in the team to meet Leeds. That much was crystal clear in my mind before David worsened the problems between us when we met on the Saturday by making me lose my temper badly, something I hadn't done in years. At first he simply refused to accept he had anything to answer for and that made me blow up.'

One result of that, at least, was to bring out the predators from rival teams who still wanted to get their hands on David. 'I note with interest that Sir Alex Ferguson and David Beckham seem to have a difference of opinion that has not gone away,' commented Joan Gaspart, the newly elected president of Barcelona. AC Milan, having tried at least twice that summer to buy David, also pricked up its ears.

Martin Edwards, chairman of United, stepped in to quash rumours about both David and his teammate Paul Scholes. 'There is no way we would allow them to go,' he snapped. 'They are the backbone of this team and we want them to remain at United. We would be extremely reluctant to see either player leave.'

David maintained a diplomatic silence. He could afford to.

Just for once it seemed that Fergie was unwise, to put it mildly, to bring up that row again, especially after both had gone to such lengths to publicly avow it was all over. Fergie himself felt vindicated as far as the row itself was concerned, as it made David spend more time in Cheshire. But once more it had highlighted David's new-man qualities, his willingness to step away from the traditional image of a footballer and his love of his family. And now he was about to stun everyone yet again when he publicly welcomed his new role – that of gay icon.

CHAPTER 8

GLAD TO BE – EH?

And so, David, asked the interviewer brightly, how does it feel to be a gay icon? No one who knew David would have been surprised by the answer. 'Actually, I think it's cool,' he said. 'Other people may have a problem with it, but whether men or women fancy you, it's always nice to be liked. I think it's great.'

It went on. When did David first become aware of the attention from gay men? 'I was getting mentions in magazines like *Attitude* as soon as I started playing for Manchester United,' said David. 'Obviously you get a bit of stick from other footballers about things like that because football is supposed to be such a macho game. There's that attitude of "I'm a footballer, I go down the pub, drink beer." But I've never been that type of person. I prefer to go to a nice restaurant or bar with my wife. That's my perfect night out.'

Had David ever been sucked into that kind of laddishness? 'No not at all,' he said. 'Of course, I've tried it – I've gone out and tried drinking loads, eating an Indian and throwing up but it didn't suit me. Not as a person and certainly not as a husband.'

David was then asked if he'd ever been chatted up by gay men. 'Yes, a couple of times,' said David cheerfully. 'We go to gay bars – not every week, but quite a bit, so I get a bit of that. I've had wolf whistles from blokes as well. It doesn't bother me and Victoria thinks it's cool.'

Victoria herself revealed how much her husband revelled in his new-found status. 'He's a big flirt and he loves it,' she said to DJ Jeremy Joseph on his *G-A-Y* show on radio station Spectrum. 'He walks around the kitchen saying, "I'm a gay icon, I'm a gay icon", and when I try to say, "So am I," he just goes, "But they love me, you've got nothing on me, baby."'

It is a rare man, let alone footballer, who could have come out with that, but it was typical of David. For the fact is that he is so secure in his own sexuality – and he and Victoria have a very passionate love life as in that same interview she talked about him being an animal in bed – that he is able to accept compliments from both sexes without batting an eyelid. It is the same quality that allows him to wander around in sarongs, wear nail varnish and have his wife go on television in Japan to tell the world that he likes facials. David simply doesn't care what other people think. He minds when he gets hatred on the football pitch, as would anyone, but, off the pitch, he goes his own way.

Very rarely, David goes too far and has to be hauled back for his own good. A case in point was at that time: David was sporting a skinhead look but what he had really wanted was to have a Mohican haircut. Sir Alex put his foot down and made David shave it off. 'I couldn't have it, which I was gutted about because it looked wicked,' David said sadly. 'But the manager didn't think I needed the publicity or a slaughtering in the papers for the next week.

'I watched the film [*Taxi Driver*] the other night and thought, That's wicked, so I got Tyler [David's hairdresser] round to do it. We were in the changing room before the game and he [Sir Alex] turned to me and asked, "Are you going to shave it off?" To be fair, he wasn't nasty about it – he just said I didn't need the abuse – and at the end of the day I don't. He was only really looking out for my best interests, I think. I suppose in a way I wanted to keep it and I would have if he hadn't said anything. But he's the boss and sometimes you've got to listen to him. Well, *most* of the time.'

David's maturity, noticeable even when he was a teenager, would have led to his inner security whatever way his life had gone, but his marriage to Victoria only served to heighten it. The couple's closeness and devotion to each other is not, alas, to be found in many relationships and he knew it. 'Our relationship is the sort that most people don't have and one I think most people would love to have,' David said simply. 'I think people like to see the way we act!

'It's not just a thing we do in front of the cameras. We go

out, we hold hands. We're always holding hands, you know – whatever. Even if it's watching a film we're always holding hands or cuddling. That's the way we've always been and, in a lot of ways, I think people like to see that – it's that fairytale thing. Maybe we'll get slaughtered for it but it's not for show, it's for real. We love each other so much it hurts. It's at that stage where we don't do things for publicity, we do it because we're like that at home. We're like that when we're watching telly. We do it all the time.'

David was absolutely right. He had summed up exactly why the public are so interested in the two of them. An ancient Greek philosopher once said that, when human beings first peopled the world, they had four arms, four legs and cartwheeled around in a state of bliss. But the gods were jealous of their happiness and so split them in half and ever since then humans have been destined to wander the world, searching for that lost other half. Some find it, some don't. David and Victoria did.

But David's closeness to Victoria meant it was inevitable he would take a step back from his parents. 'I was definitely a mummy and daddy's boy for a long, long time,' said David. 'I was dependent on my mum and dad in all ways, whereas I think later I learned other things and grew up. Since I've met Victoria, I've done that a lot. I've not been as dependent on my mum and dad, and whoever else I depended on in the past. I love my mum and dad and they're always going to be there for me. But it's the same with them, I'm sure. At a point in their lives, they turned round and needed each other more than their own mums and dads. But you always need your mum and dad, whatever.'

David is also far more intelligent than he is usually given credit for. His misfortune is his voice: it is soft and whispery rather than deep and resonant and so tends to belie his actual words. But, if you read what David is saying rather than listen to him, it's clear that he has an inner maturity and intelligence that a great many people do not possess. Apart from anything else, you do not achieve the fame and riches that David has without some sort of inner quality and, if, say, he had a voice like Stephen Fry, he would come across as witty and self-deprecating rather than a bit 'not all there'. But, being David, even this failed to bother him.

As the new football season approached, there was a noticeable change in the fans' attitude. There was a sense that they had gone too far during Euro 2000 and almost seemed to be trying to make it up to him. At a pre-season match in York, the fans actually cheered him as he ran out on to the pitch, much to David's own bemusement. 'It was nice to get a good reception at York,' he said. 'In pre-season last year I was getting booed here and there, but it made a nice change at the weekend.'

David's new-found popularity went straight to his pocket. Well aware that rival clubs would grab him the moment they could, it was rumoured that United offered to raise David's pay packet to £80,000 a week. 'David will be here for as long as I'm manager,' said Ferguson. 'He's not pushing for any new negotiations on his contract and he's looking forward to the new season.' But he did hint that there might be a pay rise at the end of the season.

Kevin Keegan helped matters further when he hinted that David could become England captain. Autumn was turning into a gruelling time for Beckham – Victoria was upset when her single only got to Number 2 and she then went on to contract meningitis while touring in Europe. David had to cope with all that on top of his footballing career, but he carried on as normal, impressing the England manager with his coolness and determination. 'I would definitely say that one day David could captain England, but there are processes to go through,' he said. 'He might not be the most vocal of players but he's got leadership qualities.'

Jackie Adams moved Victoria and Brooklyn to Goff's Oak, so David could fly to Paris with the England squad for a friendly game against France, followed by the European and World Championships. There were the usual rumours about the possibility of his moving abroad, the usual round of denials from everyone and then, in October, the publication of *Beckham: My World*, a sort of coffee-table volume full of pictures of, well, David. It also contained a few telling insights about his life. David revealed that he would love to go skiing when he eventually stops playing football as he can't currently do so because of the insurance, and that he would love to fly to the moon one day, were it ever possible.

He also talked about building a football pitch at the new

home in Hertfordshire and having horses. 'The new house is perfect for a five-a-side pitch for me and Brooklyn,' he wrote. 'I'd like us to have three or four more babies. That would keep me busy.' And there was every chance that they would do so, given that he went on to write, 'I'm often asked whether scoring a goal is better than sex. For me there is no contest. Of course, sex is better.'

And, of course, the book was a best-seller. As the hostility created by the 1998 match against Argentina died away, it was replaced by straightforward hero worship. David turned up at Manchester's Trafford Centre for a book signing, where he was mobbed by a crowd of thousands; it included teenage girls crying, 'I'd die for you, David,' and parents lifting their children above the heads of the crowd to get a glimpse of the great man. 'It's mad,' said one of the security guards present. 'There's been nothing like this since the Irish singer Daniel O'Donnell was here.'

With all of this adulation going on and a book to publicise, it was almost inevitable that David would end up on *Parkinson*. Wearing a black suit and a pair of sparkling diamond earrings, he took the opportunity to address some of the more telling issues of the day. 'I can actually say I have not worn Victoria's knickers – not in public, anyway,' he said. 'It will be a bit worrying if I did because she is smaller than me. When Victoria starts talking, sometimes she can't stop. She says things that get a bit of coverage but I love her still, so it doesn't matter.'

Victoria was there, hidden in the wings with Brooklyn, while about 30 of David's family and friends, including his parents, sisters and parents-in-law were in the audience to give David a bit of confidence. 'David was in knots about appearing on the show,' said a friend. 'He wanted to look out there and see as many friendly faces in the audience as possible.'

There was also something different about his voice. Onlookers thought he might have taken elocution lessons to deepen it slightly.

Rather ironically, given what was to happen, David also said that he did not feel the need to move abroad to become the best possible player. 'I don't believe that to reach my coming of age as a player I would have to move to the Italian or Spanish leagues,' he said. 'A lot of people say that you must move to Spain or Italy to become one of the best, or to prove yourself, but I don't believe that. I feel that I will stay in England as long as my family are happy and I am happy. The moment that changes, I will look at my options. But, if I am playing good football and getting headlines on the back pages, then I am happy. The press likes to say that Victoria wears the trousers and makes the decisions. But, at the end of the day, if I do leave United, it will be my choice, not Victoria's. As a family man I have to look at what will be best for the family. It will not be Victoria who says, "You have got to leave Manchester United because I want better shops in Milan or whatever."'

David also talked about Euro 2000, explaining that he, too, had found it to be a turning point with regard to the fans.

Asked about flicking his finger he said, 'My reaction could have been far worse. You would have had to be a saint not to be hurt by the things being said about my wife and son. Oddly enough, after that people came out and supported me. They knew I didn't deserve that kind of treatment. It had been happening to me for two years, yet some people didn't believe it until they heard it in the summer. I think it shocked them to realise what I'd had to put up with. I get abuse even when I'm walking down the street. People shout, "Beckham, you are a so-and-so." It is not very pleasant for me and my family.'

Victoria helped him to cope, not least by pointing out that the fans who scream abuse are almost certainly jealous of David and his life. He was, after all, living many a young man's dream: sporting superstar, extremely wealthy and with a collection of cars that included Ferraris and Range Rovers. 'Victoria has always said to me, "They are getting their aggression out on you and going home to probably a sad life,"' he revealed. 'She always turns around and says that, if you are ever at that point [of lashing out] just think about what you've got and what you are doing. These people would do anything to play for Man United and England. I've got to think of that straight away or I could do something.'

Beckham had matured to the extent that he was even able to look back on the worst time of his life, after the match against Argentina in 1998, and say he'd gained something from it. For a player who was fundamentally mature but who had a tendency to lash out, in many ways it was the making of him. David had to learn to curb his temper both on and off the pitch, while receiving a level of abuse that would have destroyed a lesser man. But that which does not destroy you makes you stronger – and David was now at a stage where he was even ready to captain England.

My World continued to sell well – embarrassingly so. David did a book signing in London with Victoria and Brooklyn in attendance (all the critics who thought Victoria shouldn't have dragged him around with her when her record was released should note it worked both ways) and 8,000 fans turned up to get their signed copy. Signed copies of Sir Alex Ferguson's autobiography were also on display – and sold only 500. 'We get queues for all book signings by famous people, but the turnout for Beckham is certainly the biggest.'

A further insight into the couple's lifestyle came when Victoria gave an interview to *Q* magazine, in which she described him as an 'obsessive compulsive'. 'He's got that obsessive compulsive thing where everything has got to match,' she said. 'He's got it, like, ridiculously. If you open our fridge, it's all co-ordinated down either side. If there are three cans of Diet Coke he'd throw one away rather than having three because it's uneven.' Clearly the tidy teenager who had lived with Annie and Tommy Kay had grown even more fastidious in his habits over the years.

And, of course, the thorny subject of the knickers came up again. 'I do often say things I shouldn't, but that's my personality,' Victoria confessed. 'When I said the thing about him wearing my knickers … I'd never say anything to purposely make it difficult for him. I have learned my lesson but, in interviews, I am quite an honest person. I've got a dry sense of humour and I say things and unfortunately most of the media don't have a sense of humour. As if he'd fit in my bloody underwear! I'm a size six.

'But he's a very strong personality, David. He would never do anything he didn't want to. People think he's some kind of idiot and Posh Spice says to him, "Oh, put on this skirt, David, it'll look really great." And then he goes out looking like a prat. He's really not like that. He's a good-looking bloke, he's got the body to wear whatever he wants to wear and look amazing in it. And he loves it. If he didn't love it, he wouldn't dress like that. It's nothing to do with me.'

In October another dream came true: David was named as England captain as England prepared to play Italy in Turin. 'This is one of the proudest moments in my footballing career,' he said. 'When I was a kid, I used to dream about leading England out.'

England coach Peter Taylor, in charge for just this match, was in no doubt that Beckham was the right man for the job. 'He deserves to be captain,' he said. 'He'll take the responsibility on board, he'll respond to it and I hope in the right way. He has matured greatly since the 1998 World Cup. He is a marvellous player and I think he will handle the responsibility of leading the team. He looks like he desperately wants to play for Manchester United and England, that he loves his football and I intended to give him the captaincy from the moment the FA asked me to take charge for this one-off game. All the other players respect David and I see no reason why he can't go on and captain England for many years to come.'

Victoria was equally delighted for her husband. 'I'm really proud of him,' she said. 'He has worked really hard and I know he will be a fantastic captain. I'm so glad he has been given this chance.'

It almost goes without saying that David took his new responsibilities seriously. 'I won't stand up and give a speech but it's my job to go up to players and talk to them,' he said. 'I'm not used to doing that because I'm quite shy. It'll be hard for me but I've got to learn to do things like this and I'm sure I'll do it. It's exciting because everyone's talking about the new era – it's great for me to be captain and to lead the team out. I've been quieter than some of the other captains – I won't be shouting. But I can give different things to the team.'

David was also looking forward to playing in midfield. 'I've got to change my game and talk to other players but hopefully I'll be able to do that,' he said. 'I'm pleased I'm playing in the centre as a captain because it'll give me more of a chance to speak to players a bit more and keep the team going. I know everyone will give 110 per cent – but to get a good result over here is really hard. Victoria wanted to come but she's working, though I'm sure she'll watch it on the telly. But my mum and dad will be here – it's going to be a proud moment for them.

Top: One of the world's greatest footballers, as a child, with his mum and dad who are already proud of his up-and-coming skills.

Bottom left: A young David Beckham collecting an award at Old Trafford in 1986. Bobby Charlton stands over him.

Bottom right: Within the boy's frame – a remarkably mature determination to succeed.

Top left: Becks keeping up on the sports pages whilst in Spain on a trip he won to the Barcelona FC youth academy with the Bobby Charlton Soccer School. To his right is Stuart Leigh.

Top right: On the same trip to Barcelona, with Terry Venables.

Bottom: A very little David is the first on the left in the front row. His father stands, in blue, clapping on the back row.

p: David Beckham joins Manchester United on the day of his 14th birthday. *s* family and Alex Ferguson stand in the background.

ottom: Young but already powerful – Beckham in flight.

Top left: David with Eric Cantona. During this time, David was lodging with Annie and Tommy Kay in Manchester.

Top right: The Kay's house where David lived between the ages of 16 and 21.

Bottom: Beckham making his league debut for Manchester United against Leeds United

vid Beckham's was a swift rise – here he is seen carrying the 1997 P.F.A. Young
ayer of the Year cup.

There's only one David Beckham! David celebrates scoring for England in the 1998 World Cup against Colombia.

Top: The man in action. Yet another Beckham goal, this time against Chelsea.

Bottom left: The perfect gentleman off the pitch, David's passionate relationship with football has sometimes got him in trouble whilst on the grass. Here he vents his frustration at referee Gerald Ashby during a match against Leicester City.

Bottom right: Five great footballers (*from left*): Ryan Giggs, Denis Irwin, Teddy Sheringham, David Beckham and Andy Cole, all in the famous Man U red.

The post-match meeting in Old Trafford that was to lead to one of the most publicised romances of our time.

My dad's always watched England games, so to see me leading the team out will be a special moment for him. Two years ago, if someone had turned round and told me that in two years I would be England captain, I would have said, "I don't think so." I've got a lot of respect for Kevin Keegan as a man and a manager. I've got a lot to thank him for.'

It was the fulfilment of a dream, but as yet it was unclear how long David would be England captain. It had just been announced that Sven-Göran Eriksson was to be the new England manager and his thoughts about the captaincy were as yet unknown. But, if David was worried, he chose not to show it. Instead he decided to have another tattoo – this time the name Victoria, spelled out in Arabic on the inside of his left arm.

'I tried it in Chinese the other night and drew some characters,' he said. 'It looked good and Victoria was impressed but I copied it off a Chinese menu so I probably had "fried rice, salt and pepper ribs and hot and sour soup" on my arm instead of "Victoria"! I've wanted a new tattoo for ages, but we agreed it would look a bit tacky if I just had "Victoria" in English. So I've finally gone for Arabic because it's quite arty and I wanted something different. This is what I do when I'm bored – new tattoos, new cars, new watches. I sound like a right sad git.'

The new tattoo coincided with the release of a documentary video, *The Real David Beckham*, and again, if you read what David says rather than listen to him, he comes across as clever and witty. Here he is on the way to film *Parkinson*: 'It's an honour to be invited on his show because he's a legend. Everyone tries to catch me out and most of the time I do get caught out. He'll probably throw in a couple of long words that I don't understand. I'll just have to combine the little words that he says before that and make something up.' If that speech had been delivered in a Stephen Fry-esque baritone, it would have come across as witty and self-deprecating. But once again, poor old David's voice let him down.

He also revealed that he knew Sir Alex was not totally delighted with his lifestyle. 'Alex Ferguson would like me to go straight home from training, but I think he realises that doesn't happen any more,' he said. 'I like doing photo shoots because you can order pizza and McDonald's.' David was pretty unique in that, too. There can't be many models who feast on fatty food when their picture's being taken.

He also referred to the row over missing training when Brooklyn was ill. 'A lot of players have learned over the years, if you get on the wrong side of Alex Ferguson, it's not nice,' he said.

Sir Alex himself had his say. 'What David has to control is the publicity machine from Victoria's side – it has been interfering with his life and you can't have that,' he said. 'You are a footballer, your wife's job is different to yours. There is nothing worse than when you pick up a paper and see, "Oh Christ, where is he now?" I think he's tried hard to make sure that's under control a bit. Since that little argument, there's been better dialogue.'

But not, of course, for long. David was prepared to rein in his new lifestyle to a certain extent, but he was growing increasingly used to the trappings of fame, and fame is addictive: once you've got it, you don't want to give it up.

But equally, David put his fame to good use. As Christmas approached, the couple visited Christie Hospital in Manchester, where they spent an hour distributing presents to children. It was an extremely generous gesture.

'The youngsters were thrilled,' said a spokesman for the Youth Oncology Unit. 'It's something they will never forget. David and Victoria asked for the visit to be kept quiet. They didn't want any publicity, but they made everyone's Christmas.'

David remained popular elsewhere, too. The ever-hopeful Barcelona popped up again, offering David a deal worth £100,000 a week. Ryan Giggs, Andy Cole, Dwight Yorke and Jaap Stam were also seen as potential defectors to other clubs. Sir Alex wasn't having any of it. 'I would put my life on them staying, as long as we look after them,' he said. 'Nothing is certain in life, but I don't think they want to leave Old Trafford. The important thing is to be top of the league on 1 January. If we are, we will be delighted.'

Christmas approached – David was spotted buying sexy underwear for Victoria at the exclusive London shop Agent Provocateur – and the family spent it with Victoria's parents at Goff's Oak. David's present to Victoria was generous, to put it mildly – a £300,000 state-of-the-art recording studio in Beckingham Palace. David presented her with architects' plans and explained he was having it built so that he and Brooklyn could come in to listen, and so that Victoria wouldn't be kept in London so late at night. Victoria was in tears at the gift.

In the new year, negotiations began over a new contract, with David reportedly turning down an opening offer of £80,000 a week. Under Victoria's guidance, it was believed that David was determined not just to achieve pay parity with his teammates, but to be paid better than the rest of them. Not everyone was thrilled that Victoria was involved in negotiations, not least the former Nottingham Forest boss Brian Clough. 'I'm watching David Beckham with great interest these days,' he said. 'I think he's at a personal crossroads where his great talent and professionalism may collide with his lifestyle. Beckham is a highly talented player who plays for the team and Alex Ferguson has done a brilliant job with him. When necessary he has cracked down on him and Beckham has juggled all the social balls well.

'But what happens when Alex retires? Will the glamour of Milan and Madrid get to him? When you're young you can get away with all the whizzing around but it does catch up with you. He's a very fit lad now but, if he stops doing his stuff on match day, all that magazine and documentary trivia will rebound on him. He should sign a new, long contract with United, persuade his missus to have a few more bairns and get as much rest as he can. And, while he's at it, he should guide Posh in the direction of a singing coach, because she's nowhere near as good at her job as her husband is at his. I used to like my players to marry young, but I had no time for wives who interfered with the football – it was up to my players to control their wives. Alex Ferguson is just as old-fashioned as I am about that.'

In retrospect, reading those words, a clash between Beckham and Ferguson was inevitable. It wasn't just the differing personalities and lifestyles of the two men, it was a generational sea change. In Ferguson and Clough's young days, wives were wives who did what they were told to do. These days, relationships are more equal and, in the case of David and Victoria, exceptionally close. Telling Victoria to keep quiet and keep her nose out of it was as useful as telling water to run uphill. It just wasn't going to happen.

Clough was not the only one to voice reservations about the effect Victoria was having on her husband's career and David didn't like it. The two were highly protective of one another and quick to jump to the other's defence when they thought it was needed. So, just as Victoria spent hours telling people that David isn't thick, he was equally quick to jump on people who accused her of interfering.

'I do want to stay at Manchester United and it will be my decision and not Victoria's,' he said as speculation mounted that he was aiming to become Britain's first £100,000-a-week footballer. 'There has been a lot written about my contract talks. About how much I have been offered and when it will be decided. I have not started my contract talks yet, but I will be doing that soon. And, if I can reach agreement with the club, it is where I want to stay. This is where I have grown up. People claim she has her ideas about me moving abroad and about leaving United. People make out she's trying to pull me away from the club. But she isn't. She never has done. She loves living in Manchester and she is happy here – she always has been. But I will make my decision when I start talks with the club. It is a family decision but, at the end of the day, it will be my decision.'

The message was clear: David could look after his own career and didn't need his wife to do it for him. Nor was Victoria being pushy. But, of course, they discussed every move the other made because they are blessed with a strong and close relationship that allows them to do that. And, on top of that, David wanted to stay at Manchester United. But for how long?

CHAPTER 9

CAPTAIN BECKS

As Sven-Göran Eriksson moved in as the new England manager, speculation intensified as to whether he would keep David on as captain. Some of the other players had reservations, thinking that, at 25, David was still too young for the job. Eriksson went to Manchester to watch United play early in the year, but ironically David had been given a rest day and was attending a music awards ceremony in the South of France. He and Victoria sported matching black outfits with silver crucifixes for the night. Eriksson was unperturbed.

'I knew on Friday that David would not be playing but it doesn't matter because as a player I know him,' he said. 'And it doesn't surprise me that he is being rested. Manchester United want to win the Champions League, the Premiership and the FA Cup, and it is impossible for one player to play in all 60 or 70 games. You have to do these things. Alex Ferguson told me a couple of seasons ago that things like this are one of the secrets of United's success.'

He was guarded, though, as to whether David would retain the role of captain. 'I don't know about that. I will wait until I get all the players together,' he said. 'I haven't spoken to David yet or any of the players.'

The speculation did nothing to dent David's popularity. He signed another sponsorship deal, this time with Police sunglasses, worth £1 million, and promptly splashed out on a £185,000 Lamborghini Diablo GT, adding to an already extensive collection. (In later years Sir Elton John was heard to remark, 'I keep telling David, buy paintings, not cars.') He then returned to the football field, helping United to a 6–1 win against Arsenal, prompting more comment about being England's most gifted footballer.

Meanwhile, England's most gifted manager – Sir Alex – was preparing for retirement. It is a mark of quite how much relations deteriorated in just two years that his most vocal fan, and one who wished him to stay on, was none other than Beckham himself. 'It's impossible for anyone to try to influence Sir Alex, but I certainly want him to stay,' he said. 'You only have to look at his track record to know what he has done for Manchester United and what a loss he will be when he eventually quits. He has been the only boss I have played for since I signed for United when I was 16. It has been an absolute dream to work with the greatest manager we have ever seen in this country. I have only to look at my collection of medals and England caps to appreciate the part he has played in my career.'

It was a typically generous remark of David's and he was to have his wish fulfilled. Sir Alex did agree to stay on after all. Whether David later came to regret what he said is unlikely, but certainly, had Ferguson left when he originally intended to, David might well still be at United today.

Having established that he was staying at United for now, David and Victoria volunteered their services for something quite different – Comic Relief. The two proved conclusively that they did not take themselves too seriously and indeed had a very well-developed sense of humour when they agreed to be interviewed by Ali G. Ali G, a spoof character created by the comedian Sacha Baron Cohen, was then at the height of his popularity and it was a brave man (and woman) who would subject themselves to what proved to be a merciless grilling.

The introduction was a taste of what was to come: 'Every boy wants to be in his boots and every man wants to be in his missus. Big up for none other than Victoria and David Beckham!' Ali then kicked off by telling David, 'Now, just because it's Comic Relief doesn't mean you can speak in a silly voice,' before asking if he could sleep with Victoria. He then went on to ask David if he'd really wanted to go out with Emma Bunton, aka Baby Spice, before embarking on the most memorable exchange of the evening:

Ali G: 'So tell me, does Brooklyn like your music or is he getting a bit old for it now?'

Victoria: 'Well, yeah, he does like music, he jigs about and dances. He's also into football as well, so it's nice.'

Ali G: 'Respect, respect. So how old is Brooklyn now?'

Victoria: 'He's nearly two.'

Ali G: 'So tell me, is your little boy starting to put whole sentences together?'

Victoria: 'He's learning the bits and pieces, so yeah.'

Ali G: 'And what about Brooklyn?'

There followed barbed remarks about Victoria's weight, the future of the Spice Girls (who Ali managed to confuse with rival band All Saints) and the couple's taste in fashion, before an impassioned plea from Ali and the audience for David to strip off. 'Not even for charity,' he replied.

In all, the interview lasted 40 minutes, leaving both David and Victoria speechless at times. Afterwards the papers had a field day talking about how the two had been ridiculed, but in that they totally missed the point. The two would have known what talking to Ali G entailed and went ahead with it anyway, something many more self-important celebrities would have refused to do. In the same way, the two have admitted to laughing at the impersonations of them by Alistair McGowan and Ronni Ancona. David even once went so far as to say that they loved the sketch where David complained to Victoria that the peas were still in the pod, only to be told they were mangetouts. There aren't many people with the high profile of those two who would have been able to take the joke, but, say what you like about them, Victoria and David can. It is one of the many reasons that they can cope with their fame without going a little mad.

Shortly afterwards David played again as England captain and led the team to a 3–0 victory against Spain at Villa Park in Birmingham on his first outing under Eriksson at the end of February. Victoria, who could be seen wiping back tears, was in the crowd, holding Brooklyn.

'I was so proud of David because I know how much this means to him,' she said. 'It's the greatest honour to captain your country. When I saw him walking out with the armband leading his team as captain of England I was just completely overwhelmed and felt the tears welling up. It was really, really emotional and I had to try hard not to burst into tears. Holding Brooklyn as his dad walked out was one of the most amazing moments of my life. I was just completely filled with pride to see my husband and father of my baby leading the team.'

Of course, David was pleased, too, not least because the score gave the new England manager a very good reason for keeping him on as captain. He had been swapped at half-time, but the cool-as-ice Swede manager reassured everyone that that had been planned all along. 'The team performed well and I'm pleased, happy, proud of the performance. I know a little bit more now about the job and about the players. The spirit in the squad is very good and I'm feeling a bit warmer in the job now.'

To mark Brooklyn's second birthday, the Beckhams treated their son, United colleagues and their children to the freedom of a ball pool at a Wacky Warehouse fun pub. For the occasion, Brooklyn sported a tiny denim jacket with Chinese characters on it, almost identical to one worn by David. Champagne flowed for the adults and there was a birthday cake in the shape of a football pitch, while the children were entertained by clowns, stilt walkers, a magician and the Manchester United red devil. The couple were in fine form: they signed autographs for fans waiting outside, posed for pictures and even sent out some birthday cake. The fans loved it and sang 'Happy Birthday' to the little boy.

Slightly unsurprisingly, given this and his much-publicised adoration of his son, David was voted 'Perfect Dad' in a nationwide poll, beating Prime Minister Tony Blair, Bob Geldof, Fatboy Slim and Michael Douglas. But David was feeling jaded. Sir Alex, expressing concern that David might be losing his form, gave him the weekend off, prompting the usual speculation that this might be the end of his time with United. David travelled down south to rest and look after Brooklyn, as Victoria was recording a new album, and also took the opportunity to do some shopping, buying a new four-wheel-drive BMW. He was also spotted having dinner with Victoria in The Ivy, wearing his favourite earrings: £20,000 diamond and platinum hoops from society jeweller Theo Fennell.

But, while he was resting from United, he was still playing for England and led the team out at Anfield, home of Liverpool, against Finland. This was another risky occasion: Liverpool fans were given to jeering at United players in general and Beckham in particular, leading Sven-Göran Eriksson to make a public plea for them to unite behind the team.

David was worried, not least because Victoria was also going to be there. 'Obviously I'm concerned about any stick my family might get,' he said. 'It would be nice for my wife to be able to go to the game and not worry about getting in or out of the ground. I love her coming to watch and I'm sure she'll be there. Hopefully, becoming England captain has eased it. Over the last year it has got a lot better. We understand we will get a certain amount of stick as players. The most important thing is we get on as professionals with winning the game.'

In the event, England won 2–1, with David scoring the deciding goal. It was a brilliant performance. Nervous about the reception she would get from fans, Victoria had been watching at the hotel with Brooklyn and was ecstatic. 'Brooklyn and I couldn't stop cheering when David scored. He's my hero and I love him,' said a breathless Mrs Beckham after the match. 'It was a great game. Brooklyn loved watching his dad and was shouting and pointing when the camera was on him. I was really nervous. I'd bought loads of crisps and drinks so we could watch it on the box, and we had our fingers crossed they'd win. David played brilliantly and his goal was even better. I got a bit emotional, I was so happy for him.'

The crowd was so delighted it sang, 'There's only one David Beckham' as he ran off, while teammates, including Steven

Gerrard and Michael Owen, queued up to praise him. 'You look at David and he leads by example,' said Owen. 'It's important to have a captain who can perform like that.' More importantly still, it silenced the doubters who had wondered whether Eriksson was right to keep Beckham on as captain. His future now seemed assured.

David responded to all the rapture in typically modest style. 'I didn't hear the fans singing at the end,' he said. 'I was simply carried away in the moment, but to be told afterwards what they were chanting was just unbelievable. Brilliant. After getting off to a bad start we showed tremendous character to battle back, and when you do that I think any crowd will get behind you. I've never had to do so much talking on the pitch before. I'm not the kind of guy who goes around ranting and raving. My responsibility is to stay calm and talk to the younger players in particular. I can't believe I'm saying that. It makes me feel like an old man. But it's the captain's job to lead by example, whether he's a hard player or a player like me.'

And it meant all the more that the fans' singing had happened at Anfield. If Liverpool fans were finally prepared to cheer for David, then the events of 1998 really had been laid to rest. It also meant that Victoria would now be able to go to games to watch her husband without fear of abuse.

David's friend and teammate Gary Neville was also delighted and forecast that David would now captain England for some years to come. 'He's more assured and it's a necessity when you're made the England captain,' he said. 'All of a sudden you've got to take on more responsibility and it's not a problem for him. At 26 he's seen most things in football. There's not a lot that he's not seen: World Cups, European Championships, massive games for United. Sometimes at 25 or 26 you need that extra challenge, that extra motivation. Giving him the England captaincy will certainly have given him that and he can be England captain for years to come. Tony Adams and Alan Shearer retired and why not start afresh? The whole squad is a lot fresher, to be honest.'

It was a total, unqualified triumph for David, although he soon learned that, while Liverpool fans might cheer him on for England, it was a different story when he was playing for United. Just one week later he was back at Anfield and, while it was the first time he had played with United for some weeks now, it was not an auspicious occasion. The team lost 2–0, and taunts against Victoria were heard in the crowd. A week turned out to be a long time in football.

David was not unduly concerned: he had now officially attained the status of national hero. But tensions with his boss surfaced again after Sir Alex banned him from attending a charity awards ceremony in London with Victoria. He had been due to pick up the Sports Personality of the Year Award at the Capital FM Help A London Child appeal until Ferguson told him it was impossible to take time off at this stage of the season – despite the fact that he wasn't playing in the next two United matches.

He did, however, make it to London for Victoria's 27th

birthday at the end of April a couple of weeks later. He was wearing sparkling white trainers for the event and when pictures were published Adidas, maker of the trainers, was swamped with requests for more pairs of the shoes. They were, however, specially made for David. And, while he didn't have to buy them himself, he could certainly afford to: in the newly published *Sunday Times* Rich List 2001, the Beckhams were said to be jointly worth £30 million. Victoria, incidentally, was still ahead of David, earning £18 million to his £12 million.

David was putting his money to good use where his wardrobe was concerned. Fashion pundits might sneer, but the fans loved it: he was voted Most Fashionable Footballer in the Premiership, easily beating the likes of Rio Ferdinand and David Ginola, in the Burton Menswear League of Football Style.

Beckham celebrated his 26th birthday in trademark style: he had a new hairdo, is time a close crop on top of the head and shaved on either side. It was known as a 'step' cut and closely resembled the American GI style. Victoria, meanwhile, gave him a new pair of diamond earrings – David obligingly posed for photographers while wearing them – and the usual furore over his new appearance began.

David was a little bit taken aback by the latest fuss, asking one journalist who kept on about it, 'Do you fancy me or something?' The response was negative, but he was still asked if the style was right for an England captain. 'I don't think it matters,' he said. 'Being England captain is not about the way you look or what you do. Obviously you have to conduct yourself properly on and off the pitch but I don't think it's a problem. It's been made into more of a problem than it should be. Everyone is different. I'm not doing it to create attention. Sir Alex was fine and so, too, was Sven-Göran Eriksson. I don't think he can believe how much is being made of it. He said, if it was your right foot that was the problem, it would be different. Victoria loves it.'

And, at last, David's people sat down to work out a new contract with United. He was in no hurry to get anything resolved, not least because it was still not clear whether Ferguson would be staying on as manager. There was also the added factor that David was now worth a lot of money to United. They could choose to sell him now, if they wished, for an estimated £30 million whereas, if they waited until his old contract expired, he could walk away and they would get nothing. If they wanted to keep him, therefore, it was in their interests to get him signed up.

David was asked if he wanted to know what the situation was before deciding anything. 'Yes,' David replied, 'and as I've said already there is no rush to sign a new contract. It would be interesting to know who is coming in but I don't think the board or anyone else is going to tell me. I have two years left [on the old contract] and I will have to wait and see what goes on and what is said in the talks. The talks only started 11 or 12 days ago and I don't expect them to be completed this summer. I'm not going anywhere, though. As far as I am concerned, I will be reporting back to United at the start of the next season and the manager will be in charge. If the club did want to sell me, that would hurt. I love Manchester United. I have been here for 10 years and I have been a supporter of the club all my life. You can never say never about playing abroad, but right now United is where I want to be.'

An added complication for United was that the club now had more people to deal with: Tony Stephens, David's long-term agent, and members of the Outside Organisation who represented Victoria and, at her instigation now had David on their books, too. Again, it led to some concern over the influence Victoria was having over her husband's career – but, as long as David wanted it that way, there was not a great deal anyone could do.

And he continued to model for magazines. His latest appearance was on the cover of *The Face*, in which he appeared to be spattered with blood (it was actually soy sauce). He then suffered a real injury – a groin strain in a match against Aston Villa – after which it was feared that he would not be able to play in the crucial World Cup qualifier against Germany in Munich. This put David in such a black mood that he couldn't even speak to his father during a two-and-a-half-hour car journey, while Victoria had to endure a week of gloom. In the event, he was able to play, but felt he'd behaved so badly to everyone that he even apologised publicly. 'I was really down after the game, I couldn't speak to anyone,' he said. 'I don't think Victoria has seen me in this sort of mood before. I'm in a mood when we lose but I'm terrible when I'm injured. I'm saying sorry to her now. It has been difficult.'

To everyone's utter delight, England beat Germany 5–1, an

outstanding result and England's biggest ever win over Germany. David didn't score any of the goals – Michael Owen, in a game he'll always remember, scored three – but played beautifully, again justifying Eriksson's decision to keep him on as captain.

'It was one of the proudest moments of my life,' said Victoria, who had clearly forgiven him for grumbling. She had watched the match from Leicester, where she was performing. 'David was brilliant. He led from the front like a general and I'm not ashamed to admit I was in tears. He was under so much pressure to deliver the result England wanted. But typically he came off the pitch and congratulated everyone else. He has given the country something to shout about. They are all heroes out there.'

David was, indeed, in typically generous form. 'Everyone showed great character after we went a goal down so early on,' he said. 'We just tried to get the ball to Michael Owen and Stevie Gerrard as much as we could.'

And Sven? He was absolutely delighted – and as coolly detached as ever. 'We have to forget about this game and concentrate on the one we have on Wednesday,' he said, referring to the forthcoming match against Albania. Clearly, no one and nothing was going to ruffle him – a quality that stood him in good stead when he went on to have ructions in his own personal life.

As the scale of the victory began to sink in, it was hailed as a victory for England that was second only to the 1966 World

Cup. And David had been the captain. When the team went to change after the match, they felt as bemused as everyone else. 'We sat in the dressing room afterwards just looking at each other as if to ask, "What happened there, then?"' David revealed. 'When the world looks at the scoreline, they will be as amazed as we are.' David also said that Eriksson had offered to substitute him before the end because of that groin strain. 'Who would want to miss out on the finish of a night like that?' he asked. 'The moment I will remember most is walking over to the England fans at the end to celebrate. It was an amazing feeling. As the goals started to go in, we kept looking around at each other like we were all thinking, "What the hell is going on?" You could see it on the faces.'

But although the team were allowed a night of celebrations, the next morning it was back to England and straight back to training. Sven-Göran Eriksson might have been ice to Sir Alex Ferguson's fire, but both had exactly the same attitude when it came to keeping their teams ready and fit. After the training session, however Eriksson did allow his men, who were staying in Slaley Hall Hotel in Northumberland, some time off. Some played golf – the others went shopping.

Of course, when everyone calmed down, they realised there was still some way to go. Germany was still top of the qualifying group, with England three points behind, which meant the forthcoming matches against Albania and Greece were crucial. David was well aware of this. 'The whole nation was behind us in Germany and will be behind us in Newcastle,' he said. 'There'll be no problem about lifting the players for the Albania game, but people need to be patient. Remember it took us more than 70 minutes to score in Albania and their defence could again cause us some problems.'

As David and his teammates prepared for their next match, the extraordinary hold the Beckhams had on the affections of the country became yet more apparent with the appearance of something called The David Beckham Effect. *FHM*'s *Bionic* magazine surveyed 3,000 men throughout the UK and found that a massive 88 per cent said that love and affection, rather than beer and one-night stands, were what they wanted most from life. Of the men surveyed, 85 per cent said that sex can stay good in a long-term relationship, two-thirds said their best ever sex was with their wife and 70 per cent said they had never cheated on their girlfriend. It was a long way from laddishness – and it was all down to one D Beckham.

'The family man is cool again,' said Phil Hilton, editor-in-chief of *FHM Bionic*. 'Beckham more than anyone personifies the new dad – not the old dad who bought his clothes from a camping shop and spent his spare time in a shed on the allotment.' It is fair to say that when you start being cited as the cause for national trends, you have made your mark on the country.

David returned to *Parkinson*, this time with Victoria at his side. On the show Mrs B sang 'IOU', a song she had written for David, to which he responded by wiping away a tear. Her new album, *Not Such An Innocent Girl*, had just been released, and David loyally assured everyone that he loved it. 'It's not my kind of music, but her album has actually made it into my car,' he said. He then informed a startled Parky that he had actually contemplated killing himself when he was falsely accused of cheating on Victoria, before the lady herself lightened the atmosphere by revealing that she calls him 'Goldenballs'. The nickname stuck.

And David proved that he deserved it a week later when England played Greece, resulting in a 2–2 score. The England team as a whole were lacklustre, allowing Greece to build up to 2–1 until David single-handedly (or footedly) saved the day with an injury-time free kick to equalise the score. 'It's the best feeling ever. We didn't play the prettiest of football,' David said after the game. 'We got a goal back and then they got another one and so we had to keep on battling. For a young team to come back from 1–0 to 1–1 to go 2–1 behind and then come back to 2–2 again, it shows the character of the team and how much we all wanted it. It was a good time to score and one that had to go in. I'd had quite a few free kicks and I'd been a bit disappointed with most of them. And then when I got my chance, Teddy Sheringham said, "I'll have it," but I said it was a bit too far out for him and I fancied it. We kept on battling and we got our just desserts in the end. We wanted to go to the World Cup finals and we are there now.'

Even the normally cool Sven-Göran Eriksson was carried away, racing down on to the pitch to congratulate his team. 'I'm very happy today, of course,' he said. 'It was a marvellous afternoon because we didn't play that well, especially in the first half. The Greeks deserved 1–0 at half-time. The second half we did much better and showed a lot of character. We were a bit unlucky they scored again. It was a marvellous end to a football game. Beckham scored the goal and it was really deserved. It wasn't a winning goal but a drawing goal, which was enough. He played one of the best games I have seen him play. He ran all over the pitch. He was a big captain and if we want to do well in the World Cup, we must do that again. He did everything today to push the team to make us win the game. That was the first step to something that could be very beautiful. Let's be happy today, tomorrow let's try to be better.'

As was becoming usual these days, the whole country cheered Beckham for his performance. England fans danced round Trafalgar Square, singing, 'There's only one David Beckham'. There were tributes from everyone, including, of course, Victoria, who was in Italy. 'I told you David was called Goldenballs – and today he showed the whole world why,' she crowed. 'I am so proud of him and the whole team. I was in tears when I phoned him up after the game. It's going to be so exciting going to the World Cup. I won't see him for a week as I'm on tour in Europe, but I'll be having a drink for him tonight!'

David celebrated by taking his parents, parents-in-law, son, sister-in-law, her daughter and assorted others to dinner at the Indian restaurant Shimla Pinks in Manchester. The chef made a surprise cake for him and the whole restaurant gave him a standing ovation when he blew out the candles. 'I think David was genuinely surprised by the reception he got,' said the restaurant's owner, Nisar Khan. 'And he made sure he thanked the other customers by asking us to hand a piece of cake to everyone. That is the type of person he is. He wanted everyone to enjoy the moment and share in the celebration.'

It was hardly surprising that the jubilant David went on to say that he wanted to play in every game he could. Sir Alex wanted to rest him during United's forthcoming match against Olympiakos, but David persuaded him otherwise. 'I don't want a rest, particularly when things are going so well,' he said. However, Fergie did manage to get Beckham to take a weekend off, which he spent jetting to see Victoria, who was now in Scandinavia. And who can blame him for such overexcitement? To go from villain to national treasure – there were even calls for him to be knighted – would please anyone and David, a modest and emotional man, found it especially overwhelming.

He also made peace with Germany by appearing on a chat show with Victoria. For the occasion he wore a £20,000 watch, a £15,000 ring and £5,000 earrings – even more jewellery than Victoria was wearing. 'I'm just a regular bloke,' insisted David, before winning the hearts and minds of the audience when he was asked about German coach Rudi Voller. 'He's an excellent professional, a great guy and a great footballer.' That one was greeted with wild applause. David looked ready to conquer the world.

CHAPTER 10

THERE'S ONLY ONE DAVID BECKHAM

As Christmas approached, Manchester United had still not come to an agreement with David over his contract. This was becoming a real problem. Christmas had been set as an informal deadline for the talks and, if a deal were not sorted out by then, there was a real possibility that United would sell David the following summer, when he had a year left to run. For a start, there was disagreement about the money involved and, on top of that, SFX favoured a mere two-year extension. United sources claimed that they were near to fixing terms but, interestingly, David had actually started asking colleagues about life abroad. It seems that, as far back as the end of 2001, he was beginning to realise where his future might lie.

But he was still England captain and as such he had responsibilities to pursue – sartorial ones. Much to the amusement of onlookers, Sven-Göran Eriksson had asked him to dress the England side for the World Cup, prompting much ribaldry about sarongs. David responded with dignity. 'It's my job as England captain to organise things like the suits and pick the colour and style of them,' he announced. 'Normally the manager has a say but Mr Eriksson said, "Let him do it." They won't be anything like the Liverpool cream suit or anything flash either. They will be very normal.'

Given David's status as national treasure, it was almost inevitable that he would be named BBC Sports Personality of the Year for 2001 – and he was. More than 750,000 people had voted: Beckham, dressed as a Chicago gangster, dutifully thanked his family, Sir Alex, Eriksson and, of course, Victoria and Brooklyn. It was a generous gesture. David had again been dropped from the United line-up against West Ham – and United had lost. There had been some muttering that, had David been included, the outcome would have been different, but no one was in the mood to spark yet another public row. In fact, David went on to say that Fergie had been right to drop him.

The very next day, David won another award: Britain's Best-Dressed Man, beating the likes of Robbie Williams and Jude Law in a poll of *Heat* magazine readers. Shortly after that, he was runner-up for the FIFA World Player of the Year awards for the second time in three years, losing narrowly to Real player Luis Figo. But still the rumblings of discontent went on. Despite his public statement, David was said to be increasingly angry that Ferguson kept dropping him. United, meanwhile, claimed that David had a bad back – and there was speculation that the real cause of the problem was the amount of money David was demanding. David was sanguine. He went shopping.

Christmas passed with no resolution to the problems, which promptly resurfaced in January. Sir Alex put David on the starting line for the first time in seven weeks in a match against Fulham, but Beckham was not at his best, and was dropped again in the next match with Newcastle. He kept publicly stating that he wanted to stay at United, but observers were beginning to ask, if he was never going to play, what was the point? Sven-Göran Eriksson wasn't happy, either. He would not have dreamed of criticising Sir Alex publicly, but an England player needs to play and David was not getting much chance to do so at the moment.

And the problem with the contract had still not been resolved. United were aware that, if they didn't tie David down by January 2003, he would be free to sign a pre-contract agreement with another club, but the various advisers simply could not agree. There was not only the money to think about, there were also lucrative image rights. 'Both sides are frustrated,' said Peter Kenyon. 'You do reach a point where you can't go further and after several months of good negotiations you also reach a point where you conclude things one way or the other.' The other, of course, referred to selling David.

David played on. Victoria, meanwhile, admitted that actually she had had some influence on her husband's fashion sense and particularly disliked the way he wore his trousers high up his body. 'It was a case of, "Those trousers, what size are they, sir? Aren't they irritating your nipples?"' she said. 'Me and Britney [Spears] can both pick men that aren't really that great [Britney was at the time dating Justin Timberlake], change the clothes, change the hair and they're pin-ups.' It was not the timeliest of interventions. The last thing that David needed at this stage in the game was yet more speculation that it was actually Victoria who was in charge.

There was at least one step forward in February 2002 when, after months of speculation, Sir Alex Ferguson confirmed that he would be staying on as manager. 'I am over the moon. We had been hearing the rumours about the manager not retiring, but we didn't believe them,' said David. 'But he came in before training on Tuesday and told us.' It emerged that Sir Alex's wife Cathy had persuaded her husband to stay on. 'We all know about wives always making the decisions!' chirped David. He also revealed that negotiations were finally moving forward with his own contract. A salary of £70,000 a week had been agreed and now the two teams had just to sort out image rights.

It was at this point that it was sadly revealed that David's parents were divorcing. Sandra had started the proceedings the previous October, but it was only now that the split became public. His parents had been together for 32 years and David was distraught. He went to pay them a secret visit. 'David is terribly upset because he adores his mum and dad,' said a friend. 'He went to see them this weekend because he wanted the chance to speak to them and see if he could smooth things over to some extent. David is a realist – he knows if the situation has gone as far as the court then there's not much hope of them getting back together. But he is finding it very hard seeing them not getting on with each other so much.' Indeed he was. For a man who was so famously happily married, it was a dreadful wrench to see his parents at war.

In his autobiography he described his parents' marriage and that might have given a clue as to the reason for the split. 'Dad loves my mum,' he wrote. 'But he's never been affectionate to her in front of my two sisters and me and cooks only once in a blue moon. He's quite hard-faced and can be sarcastic. He also gets fired up easily. If something is said about me, he'll want to punch whoever said it. If my mum hears it, she'll just want to cry. The quality I least like in myself is my short temper. I think I got it from my dad.' Clearly David's marriage, full of affectionate gestures all the time and one in which he played an equal role around the household, was very different from that of his parents.

However, nothing – even this personal trauma – could put a stop to the Beckham bandwagon and David's latest £1-million venture was announced at the end of February: he was to design clothes for Marks & Spencer. It was to be a range of boys' clothes and who better than Beckham, with his joint love of football and fashion, to be linked with it? 'David Beckham is the perfect icon for this boyswear range,' said Michele Jobling, the project's managing director. 'Not only is he the number-one sporting hero but he is also a great style icon and role model – we are thrilled to have him on board.'

David was clearly delighted with his new role. 'For some time now,' he said in a statement, 'I have been enjoying the creative side of my commercial work and, when Marks & Spencer offered me the opportunity to actively assist in the design of clothing for youngsters, I was delighted. I want to help create the kind of clothes I would have worn as a youngster.'

It was turning out to be an action-filled year for David. Hardly had the dust settled on the announcement when there was more excitement. Victoria was expecting a second baby and another announcement followed. 'This has been such an exciting year for us – England are in the World Cup finals, Victoria's had a second Top 10 hit and now we are expecting a new baby,' it read. 'It's fantastic. Brooklyn is really looking forward to having a little brother or sister to play with.'

Indeed, both families were delighted. David's father Ted was in Manchester to watch United play Aston Villa and drove Victoria to the game. 'I wouldn't have thought this will be the end of it,' he said as the family prepared for a champagne celebration. 'Victoria has said she would like a lot of children and I know David would, so I'm sure there will be more.'

Sandra might have been estranged from him but she agreed. 'We're all really thrilled about the baby and I can't wait for it to be born,' she said.

There were similarly supportive remarks from the Adams family. The dynasty was set to continue.

And it was celebrated in a slightly unusual fashion. Sikh twins Amrit and Rabindra Singh painted a picture of the family, representing them as Hindu gods. David, complete with four arms, was Shiva; Victoria, wearing a cocktail dress and holding a microphone, was the mountain goddess Parvati; and little Brooklyn was their son Ganesh. The painting went on display in Manchester, with the twins explaining, 'They are figures people follow just like gods in the Hindu religion. It is not blasphemous.'

An image of David also appeared in Madame Tussaud's in a new attraction called Goal! He had finally caught up with Victoria, who had made it to the waxwork museum three years earlier.

The announcement of the pregnancy also meant that David was keener than ever to stay at United, as this was not the time to cause upheaval. 'United is the only environment I've known,' he said. 'I have so many friends around me it's difficult to imagine how I might react to anything else. I'm talking about real friends here, not just workmates.'

Sir Alex was equally eager to finalise contract details and David continued to pay tribute to him. 'Of course, I respect him because, for a start, he's the reason I'm here,' he said. 'And that goes for a lot of the other players here as well. I think we all realise that, without Alex Ferguson, we might not have progressed in the way we have. He's the one who gave us a chance and had faith in us. He believed he had some youngsters who could come all the way through. I think our respect for him stems from that. In spite of what anyone says, there's never been a problem on that score.'

The couple celebrated Brooklyn's third birthday in typically lavish style: they threw a £3,000 bash at Manchester's Printworks Complex and laid on a private screening of *Monsters Inc*, followed by clowns, conjurors and a huge birthday cake iced in the colours of Manchester United. As before, the party was attended by a number of David's teammates and their children, while the birthday boy and his father had double cause for celebration. David was voted Britain's Best-Dressed Man in a poll by *GQ* magazine – while Brooklyn also made the list at number 17.

David and Victoria were in party mode. They followed Brooklyn's celebrations with the announcement of a World Cup party, themed 'White Tie and Diamonds', to be held in May at Beckingham Palace. And contract negotiations were at long last complete: David was to receive a £70,000-a-week salary, with a further £20,000 a week for his image rights. It was a relief for everyone. David was now tied to the club for the foreseeable future – on top of which he was now one of England's best-paid footballers.

As the World Cup approached, all eyes centred on David's every move on the pitch. There were serious fears that he might have been badly injured when he was tackled by Diego Tristan during a match against Deportivo La Coruna and had to be stretchered off the pitch. This came right after Sven-Göran Eriksson warned, 'Injuries are the only big worry that I have. If I go to games and see a player on the ground I just cross my fingers.' David's injuries, however, proved less serious than originally thought, with Ferguson commenting, 'He could be back next week.'

It was a relief all round. David had matured so much, both as a person and a player, that playing without him would have been a serious blow. 'I think it would have been a big problem if he was not fit to lead England in this summer's finals,' said England legend Sir Tom Finney. 'He is one of the biggest influences on the rest of the side. He doesn't get involved in silly things like he used to.'

World Cup star Ray Wilkins agreed. 'We would really have suffered without him,' he said. 'He has proved over the last few games that he is a real lucky talisman for England.'

As David recovered from his injury, he could at least console himself with the fact that he was now the richest sports star under the age of 30, overtaking the previous year's incumbent, the boxer Naseem Hamad. Together, he and Victoria were now estimated to be worth £35 million, according to the *Sunday Times* Rich List, where they came in at 962 out of the top 1,000. And he needed the good news. A week later, back playing against Coruna, he was again stretchered off with a broken foot. Beckham was in tears on the touchline before being taken off to hospital in an ambulance, accompanied by Victoria. Ferguson said he would be out for 'six to eight weeks' and was doubtful whether he would be fit enough to play in the World Cup.

After taking medical advice, it was decided that, with intensive treatment followed by a special training programme, David would be able to play, but would miss out on the remaining United games of the season. 'I do not need to find a new captain for the World Cup,' said Sven-Göran Eriksson. 'I have one already – his name is David Beckham.'

Ferguson was also more positive. 'He has a good chance of going to the World Cup,' he said. 'At this moment I'd say it's very doubtful he'll wear a United shirt again this season.'

It was ironic. At the end of the previous year, when David had wanted to play, he had been confined to the bench. Now, when Ferguson was playing him, he was stuck in a hospital bed. David himself was rueful. 'Having seen the newspapers in the last few days, the media focus seems to have been mainly around the World Cup, whereas I have been thinking about the Manchester United games I have been missing,' he said sadly. 'The season has been building up to a great finish and I wanted to play my part in another triumphant year. The messages of goodwill I have been receiving have been overwhelming – I have always said that Manchester United fans are the best in the world and times like this remind you of just how great they are. I will be joining them in the stands for the next few weeks, giving the lads every support as they try to make another great year for everyone connected with the club.'

Poor David. It was a very unfortunate accident, and a painful one at that. 'The foot was a bit sore going into the game, but that was just fluid on the foot after being tackled in the first leg the week before,' he said. 'I knew it was a bad tackle as I went into it. I felt the pain but, because we had a free kick, I jumped up to take it. But I felt it a bit and the referee made me go off the pitch. I limped off and took my boot off. I told our physio Rob Swyre to spray something on it, or put some water on it. But, as soon as he'd done that, I put my foot on the floor and felt it crack. That's when I knew it was broken. Victoria is five months pregnant, but she's the one who is running around and getting me cups of tea!'

As usual with David, his injury made the front pages – and as for it being his left foot that was broken, one supporter wrote to a newspaper saying, 'I didn't know he'd got one.' An oxygen tent was installed in the Cheshire apartment to aid David's recovery and David was given ultrasound therapy. Meanwhile, well-wishers were even leaving get-well cards around David's waxwork at Madame Tussaud's. The Prime Minister sent a good-luck message. The world, as usual, went mad.

David was not so caught up in his own problems, though, that he could not think about other people's. On the ITV programme *Tonight With Trevor McDonald* David revealed how the brave terminally ill six-year-old Kirsty Howard had moved him. Kirsty was born with a back-to-front heart and nine other cardiac abnormalities and was raising money for her hospice: so far she had raised £1,250,000 out of a hoped-for £5 million. The previous October the England team had adopted her as their mascot and a month later David and Victoria attended the hospice's annual fundraiser, the Angel Ball. 'I didn't think anyone would mean as much to me as Kirsty would until I actually met her,' he revealed. 'She is such a courageous little girl. All I can say is she touched me, she really touched me. I'm quite an emotional person, anyway, and I've certainly become more emotional since meeting Kirsty.'

Kirsty herself was thrilled to bits with her new friend. 'He came to my Angel Ball with Posh – and I didn't know,' she said. 'When they walked in everyone clapped and we had our photos taken. Then he kissed me again – that was so brilliant. I had a white dress on and a halo with tinsel. He said I looked like an angel. They came and sat with me and Mum and Dad at our table, and I sat on his lap. Posh said that I am allowed to hold his hand – but she says that she won't let any other ladies do it. That's special, isn't it?'

Kirsty was also concerned about David's broken foot. 'I've had lots of kisses off David now,' she confided. 'But I kissed him first – then he scored a goal for me and it made him happy. He makes me happy, too. When I sent him a get-well card for his foot, I wrote lots of kisses inside. I did seven because he wears the number seven on his shirt. I said, "I hope your poorly foot gets better soon." He had to go to hospital and he's got crutches. He can't run after Brooklyn, either. I've played with him and Posh gave me a Barbie doll Brooklyn got for Christmas. But if Becks takes his medicine and keeps his leg up in the air, it might be better quick and he can score another goal in the World Cup – like he did for me.' It was a typically generous gesture from David – and one that Kirsty's parents appreciated enormously.

David had now become so popular that he chalked up another first: appearing on the cover of *Marie Claire*. In its 14 years of UK existence, the magazine had only ever featured women on the cover, but was prepared to break with tradition for its June 2002 issue because it was Mr Beckham. 'When it came to putting a man on *Marie Claire*'s cover for the first time, there was only one candidate – David Beckham,' said the magazine's editor, Marie O'Riordan. 'He represents something for every woman – father, husband, footballer, icon. In a word he's the ultimate hero.'

David was also pretty pleased. 'That's what made me want to do it, because I'm the first man ever to go on the cover. I was like, "Wow!"' he said. 'I was so excited about doing the shoot.'

As ever, David came across as the consummate new man in the interview, kicking off by talking about how much he fancied Posh pregnant. 'I think it is one of the sexiest times in a woman's life when the little bump starts to appear,' he said. 'I find her really attractive when she is pregnant.' And what of the rumour that David is an animal in bed? 'That's definitely one of the true ones!' David replied.

David went on to talk about how flattered he was to be fancied by men, adding, 'I'm very comfortable with it.' This was just as well, since he was interviewed at around the same time for *GQ* magazine by David Furnish, Sir Elton John's partner. 'When I looked at Victoria for the first time I felt real love,' he said. 'People will probably go 'Ugh' and find it sickening when they hear that. As soon as I saw Victoria, that was it. When I saw the video of her wearing a catsuit in the desert, I was just, "Phwoarh".'

No one was saying 'Ugh' – rather, they were falling over themselves at how adorable David was. Could it get any better? Yes, it could. In mid-May the couple held their 'White Tie and Diamonds' party, which was an enormous success. The £350,000 bash was held in an enormous marquee in the garden at 'Beckingham Palace' and had a Japanese theme: geisha girls greeted the guests, who included Sir Elton and David F, Joan Collins and Percy Gibson, Sven-Göran Eriksson and Nancy Dell'Olio, and Jamie Oliver. Also present were Emma Bunton, Cilla Black, George Best, Mick Hucknall, Natalie Imbruglia and others too numerous to mention – including swarms of footballers, a busload of Buddhist monks and Mohammed Al Fayed, who arrived in the Harrods helicopter.

No expense had been spared for the party, the proceeds of which were to go to the NSPCC. The marquee – which covered over half an acre – was hung with lanterns and candles, and decorated with 60,000 orchids. Sushi was served, along with beef satay, monkfish, bok choi cod and stir fry. Inside, the party was split into four zones: a Japanese water garden, a nightclub, a forest and a dining area. Entertainment was provided by Beverley Knight, with Radio 1's Dreem Teem taking over in the evening.

David and Victoria themselves looked spectacular: David was wearing a knee-length button-up black jacket with sides slashed to the waist, matching trousers and sandals, designed by William Hunt. To adorn it he wore a deep red silk sash around his waist and diamond earrings. Victoria, meanwhile, was sporting a black £15,000 Ricci Burns dress. It was an off-the-shoulders design, which showed off her pregnancy-enhanced cleavage, slashed to the waist and topped off with a leather coat. The couple could not possibly have looked more radiant or more glamorous than they did that night.

'If you thought the wedding was camp, you haven't seen nothing yet,' said a jubilant Victoria. 'This is camper! David and I don't throw parties very often but when we do, we like to do it properly. At the end of the day, it is for a very serious cause, but we have to have a bit of tongue wedged into our cheek. All I have got to do is hold my shape together until the end of the party, then I can just let it all hang out. I've bought the Rolls-Royce of paddling pools. I'm just going to wallow in this thing all summer. No one is going to see me and I'm just going to swim about – it's going to be fabulous.'

Victoria was talking on a programme to mark the occasion in support of the NSPCC. David was also featured going to meet a group of youngsters at an NSPCC centre in Bow, east London. He told the children that he wanted four or five offspring of his own and that he liked rap music – but Victoria wouldn't let him play it in the car when Brooklyn was with them. He also gave them some words of encouragement. 'I have not been through half of what you've been through, but we've got to stay strong,' he told them. 'With me with the World Cup, there was a moment when I had to be strong. It's nice for me to come down here and meet you all.'

Making a speech at the party a couple of days later, David referred to meeting the children. 'Sorry for reading from the cards, it's a pretty daunting experience being up here,' he said. 'I was sat in front of 20 youngsters and every one had an attitude. Everyone was very unsure about me. To see the turnaround in the children within 20 minutes from when I first walked in – they were looking at me very strange – to laughing and joking with me. That was one of the most rewarding things I have done in my career.'

And on that positive note, the team were off to Japan for the World Cup. David had chosen Paul Smith suits for the 23 players and they all looked very smart as they trooped on to a specially chartered plane at Luton. They were also presented with goodie bags, with the contents chosen by David, containing £4,000 worth of designer luggage, state-of-the-art laptops and CD players from Sony, and silver Paul Smith cufflinks. The first stop was Dubai, where the team were to spend a few days resting with their wives and children in attendance, before going on to the Far East.

Victoria, who had been planning on staying behind, changed her mind at the last minute and decided to accompany her husband. There were still some anxieties about David's state of health, to say nothing of the fact that he had put on half a stone. David sought to allay the nation's fears. 'It is just a question of regaining my fitness now, and that's not a problem,' he said. 'I put on a little bit of weight, but it won't be a problem getting it off. There are ways of getting my fitness back other than playing in the pre-tournament games against South Korea and Cameroon.

'If I went into a tackle in one of those games, I could end up doing the same thing again to my foot. I have to be careful with it because if I do come back early there is a chance it will crack again. That's why I am taking my time. I probably could kick a ball in a week but I will leave it as long as I can. Kicking a ball won't be a problem but the first time I will take any risk with the foot is in the first game against Sweden. That's the first time I'll risk it in a tackle.'

As befitted England's best football players, the team stayed in Dubai's Jumeirah Beach Club, where junior suites – the hotel only has suites – start at £700 a night. Each came with a personal maid, dining rooms and gardens, bathrobes monogrammed with the guests' initials, swimming pools with music playing underwater – and even outside air conditioning.

The Beckhams stayed in one of the hotel's two aptly named Paradise Suites – Sven and Nancy got the other – for five days before the team itself headed on to Korea and the wives and girlfriends went back home. David and Victoria looked thoroughly miserable to be parted, hugging and kissing at the airport before engulfing Brooklyn in a family hug.

'It was like a scene from an old romantic movie,' said an onlooker. 'They seemed so sad at having to part. David looked really sad. He didn't smile once. Everyone knows he's a family man and it showed. He and Victoria had each other's hands on their knees and were really close. They kept swapping little kisses on the lips and cheek between whispering to each other. David bent down to hug Brooklyn tightly. Then he stood up and hugged Victoria. Both looked close to tears and she was very sniffy. David was really choked. You could see it in his eyes. It was as if the World Cup was miles away and he just wanted to be with his family.'

But the World Cup was just around the corner and Japan couldn't wait to welcome David. He is, if anything, an even bigger star in the Land of the Rising Sun than he is in Britain and David knew that, after the stopover in Korea, he was guaranteed the kind of welcome usually reserved for rock stars and royalty. In Japan there are over 100 websites devoted to him, he makes the covers of magazines on average seven times a week and his autograph is available in Japanese – the only European footballer to have been accorded this honour.

'I do get a lot of attention but I have never experienced anything like it is when I have been in Japan,' said David. 'It is absolutely mad. You only take one step outside your hotel room and you are surrounded by 50 people in the corridor. I tried to go shopping but they had to literally close the entire shopping centre. There were all kinds of people – kids, girls. It is nice, but mad.'

It was also all about to start again. The World Cup 2002 lay just ahead.

CHAPTER 11

BE-KA-MU

Tokyo – indeed, the whole of Japan – was going Beckham-mad. Posters of him were dotted all over Japanese buses, women's magazines featured him more heavily than ever and his number-seven strip was being bought up by thousands of young fans. They called him Be-Ka-Mu, the nearest version of his name in katakana, the system of characters used by the Japanese to describe foreign words.

The Japanese actually prefer baseball to football and so the real reason for his popularity was his appeal as a very handsome family man. 'He appeals to the Japanese because he is good-looking, well behaved and shows that he loves his wife and child,' said Monica Gillett of the British Council, Japan. 'Young people in Japan are looking to Britain and Europe for fashion and ideas. Football is the perfect answer for those who want an alternative to baseball and sumo wrestling.'

To make the point, the British Council actually circulated 200,000 pictures of Beckham on cards to Japanese children, explaining the rules of football and offering useful phrases such as 'Nice move!' and 'Get stuck in!' Crowd violence, incidentally, is almost unheard of at Japanese football matches. The fans sympathise when their team play badly, rather than hanging up effigies outside pubs.

Back in Britain, at the beginning of June, it was the Queen's Golden Jubilee weekend. England was to play Sweden on that Sunday night and Beckham sent out a message to the fans at home. 'I feel proud to be England captain and know that there are so many people back home willing us to do well,' he said. 'Everyone is patriotic about the national team and it has been proved since we qualified. It's a massive weekend. Everyone is going to have a good time and – fingers crossed – everyone will be just that little bit happier on Sunday night.'

He went on to rally his teammates. 'I've got a feeling my time has come – this will be my proudest moment in football,' he said. 'I am a patriot and to be leading out not just any England team but this England team is going to be a special moment for me. There are no nerves. We are young, talented and hungry. We've got an unbelievable spirit in the camp and only winning interests us. We want the World Cup!'

And, of course, David went on to praise Sven and the players. 'The manager helps,' he said. 'You have all seen how laid-back he is and that makes all the players feel at ease. That's good for the players. When you are young, you don't worry about the nerves. I've never been a nervous person on the pitch, you just go out and play. I can handle the pressure. When it is thrown at me, I can kick it straight back. One of Alex Ferguson's sayings is that, if you can turn round to the person next to you and feel lucky that they are there, you'll be okay. And I feel I can do that. I can do that with every one of the players out there. With the talent we have got, we can just go out and play. The expectations are high, but rightly so.'

David's parents had come out to Tokyo to cheer him on. 'This is wonderful,' said Ted. 'Now we can't wait for the real football to begin. All I can say is good luck to England and I hope David plays well.'

Victoria was being as supportive as she could be from the other side of the world, admitting that she phoned David up to 10 times a day. But the match against Sweden turned out to be something of a damp squib, resulting in a 1–1 draw. David was firmly upbeat. 'We're playing one of the best teams in the world, so we've got to believe in ourselves,' he said on the eve of the next match – against Argentina. 'That belief after the game on Sunday was down a bit. We admitted that, but we've lifted ourselves back up now. Our expectations as a team and players are very high. We've set high standards and when they drop we get disappointed.'

Pausing only to buy a kimono for Victoria, David led England out against Argentina. And this time it was personal. Four years ago, Argentina had turned David into a hate figure: now was the time for revenge – and he got it. In the 44th minute of the game, England was awarded a penalty kick, which David took. As he readied himself, the Argentinian did everything to put him off: Pablo Cavallero, the goalkeeper, shouted out where David should aim the ball, while his bête noir, Diego Simeone, shook his head gravely. David completely ignored them – and scored, ultimately leading England to a 1–0 victory.

As David scored, the Sapporo stadium erupted. So did the pubs and bars of Britain: city streets had been visibly empty while the match was on as everyone and his wife gathered to watch the match. David's redemption was complete: he was now officially the greatest living Englishman.

'It feels better than it did four years ago and it's just unbelievable,' a jubilant Beckham said after the match. 'It's been four years since the last time and a long four years. So that tops it all off.' It was difficult, he continued, 'because of the antics of the keeper telling me to put it one way and Simeone coming to shake my hand. But we've done well and worked really hard for this. The team was absolutely brilliant for the whole 92 minutes.'

The team held a party that night to celebrate at their hotel – although, mindful that there was more to come, no one drank too much and some of the players stuck to fruit juice. But spirits were high, so much so that the team broke into a rousing rendition of 'Don't Cry For Me Argentina'. Meanwhile, the hotel – the Sapporo Kita-Hiroshima Prince Hotel – laid out a huge congratulations banner and decked the reception area with St George's flags. David's parents were in attendance, while back in Britain Victoria was beside herself with joy. David had called her straight after the match and both were so excited, they later confessed, they hadn't known whether to laugh or cry.

The next day it emerged that Victoria had been worried about David taking a penalty in case it further damaged his foot. 'Just before we left to come out here, Victoria actually said, "Please don't take any penalties,"' said David. 'I said to her at that point I would definitely take the penalties. So she knew at one point I would have to but I don't think she realised it would come in the Argentina game. She watched the game with Brooklyn. I spoke to him after the game and the first thing he said to me was, "Good goal, Daddy," so that meant a lot to me.'

It had also been an extremely brave act. As David himself admitted, had he missed, against Argentina of all teams, he might well have been at square one again. But he took the risk – and it paid off.

From that moment, it got better. England went on to draw with Nigeria and then beat Denmark while, to the additional delight of England fans, Argentina crashed out of the World Cup. David's young friend Kirsty Howard sent him a good-luck letter, prompting a return telephone call from David to thank her for bringing him luck. England were now through to the quarterfinals and there seemed a real chance that they would pull through to the very end.

The outcome of the match against Denmark lifted Beckham-mania to even greater heights. More than 5,000 fans besieged the team bus to get a glimpse of David on the way to training, while the hysteria generated by his appearance meant he wasn't allowed out alone. And, unlike the other players, he didn't even have the consolation of his wife flying out to be with him. All the other wives and girlfriends were coming to Japan – Sven had promised the team this treat if they beat Denmark – except David's.

They had been apart a month now, but Victoria was seven months pregnant and it was felt it would be too risky for her to travel. Instead, the couple spoke on video link and on the phone. 'It is important she looks after herself and the baby at this stage,' said David. 'It might be a bit lonely for me, but I would rather Victoria and the baby were safe at home than me worrying about them coming over here. It's past the date when it would be safe to travel.'

It turned out that England would be playing Brazil in the quarterfinal that Friday – and it was in that match that the dream was shattered. Brazil won 2–1, leaving the entire team devastated, but especially David. He felt he'd let the country down, despite repeated assurances from everyone, including Victoria, that he'd done exactly the opposite. 'Throughout this competition, I've always had a sneaky feeling that we could go all the way,' he said sadly. 'I told everyone I had this belief we could do it. I thought we had the beating of Brazil, especially in the first half [when England scored a goal]. If we had gone in 1–0 up at half-time, who knows what would have happened? Once they got that goal, it was all a different story. It was a terribly difficult time to concede a goal. Then to leak another one straight after half-time made it even harder. In the end, it just wasn't meant to be.'

On his return to England, David cheered up a little bit. For a start, he was reunited with Victoria and Brooklyn – they had been apart a total of six weeks. And he began to realise that, far from vilifying him, the whole country was proud of its returning son. Meanwhile, his own son greeted him with the words 'I love you so much, Daddy', which did an enormous amount to lift his spirits. Indeed, he felt so much better, he was even able to get Brooklyn's name embroidered in gold on one of the back seats of his new £165,000 Bentley, his 27th birthday present from Victoria.

And, now that Beckham was back, the couple returned to their normal lifestyle with gusto. For a start, they hired some staff – and it wasn't just any old staff. John and Nicky Giles-Larkin, who were taken on to look after Beckingham Palace, had been previously employed by the late Queen Mother and had, in fact, been offered jobs by Prince Edward and his wife Sophie.

'She is delighted to have headhunted royal staff,' said a friend of Victoria. 'She knows the Palace servants are the best in the world and she wants people she can trust.' The couple were to live in a gatehouse on the edge of the Beckham's estate.

Next up, the couple decided to make a fashion statement and, when they attended the star-studded christening of Liz Hurley's son Damian at the Church of the Immaculate Conception in Mayfair, the two sported matching pink nail polish, on top of which David had gone blond. The usual media furore ensued, and even Sir Elton John, a fellow guest and someone more than capable of making a few fashion statements of his own, teased David. Beckham, as usual, took it all in good part.

Clearly planning to stay at United for many years to come, David then bought a £1.25-million barn conversion in Cheshire. With Brooklyn three years old and a new arrival expected shortly, the old flat had just become too small. The new place was just two miles away in Nether Alderley and a spectacular house: it boasted five bedrooms, a gym and a 35-foot pool, as well as half an acre of grounds. It was the perfect place to bring up a family. 'The place is amazing and absolutely ideal for raising kids,' said a neighbour.

Revelling in his new status as national icon, David then participated in the launch of the Commonwealth Games: he, Sir Steve Redgrave and Kirsty Howard met the Queen at the City of Manchester Stadium and in a glittering ceremony handed her the Jubilee Baton, which held a message from the Queen and began a round-the-world journey from Buckingham Palace in March.

As if all this were not enough, a huge painting of Beckham was then unveiled in the Pantheon, a classical building at the

Stourhead, Wiltshire, a National Trust-owned landscaped garden, as part of a month of displays and events to re-create how the gardens looked 200 years ago. The painting, by Barry Novis, showed David in full England kit, arms raised in triumph, and stood among figures including Hercules, Bacchus, Isis and Diana.

'The garden in the 18th century echoed with references to heroes and gods of the ancient world,' said Stourhead's gardener, Richard Higgs, 'a philosophy we have brought to the 21st century by placing a modern-day hero alongside these classical models.' Kathryn Boyd, a spokeswoman for Stourhead, added, 'In the 18th century these figures were a very important part of the symbolism of the arts and the English classical movement. But today we don't relate as much to them, and Beckham was chosen as a more relevant character, a dramatic analogy, a modern hero – and also as a bit of fun.'

In mid-August there was a pregnancy scare as Victoria thought the baby had stopped moving. Two weeks before she was due to give birth, David drove her to Macclesfield District General Hospital, where she was able to listen to its heartbeat.

'When she arrived she looked very worried and stressed,' said an observer. 'She couldn't feel the baby moving in the womb. When she heard the heart beating, she was so relieved she burst into tears. She was very emotional about it. All sorts of worries must run through someone's head when they are pregnant.'

Indeed, everything was fine. Two weeks later, on 1

September 2002, Victoria gave birth by Caesarian section to the couple's second son, a 7lb 4oz baby whom they called Romeo. David was present – having driven down south after playing in Manchester United's 1–1 draw with Sunderland on Wearside the previous day – and emerged from the hospital beaming. 'It's always nervous having children, but it's the most beautiful thing in the world,' he said. 'Romeo's gorgeous. Victoria's great. She's sitting up in bed and the family are here.' And why the unusual name? Because they liked it, David replied. 'Romeo looks like Brooklyn,' he went on. 'He's got Brooklyn's nose and Victoria's chin. I was there when Romeo came out. Brooklyn came in when Romeo came out.' And would David be aiming for a five-a-side team? David laughed. 'Maybe. We might work on that.'

Both sets of parents came to visit, along with Victoria's sister Louise and her husband and children. Ted was unable to contain himself. Contacted later by the press, he said, 'I don't really want to say too much at the moment. I spoke to David. He said, "Don't say anything," but I'm over the moon it's a boy. With my coaching and David's coaching, he should have a good little side there.' Victoria was 'brilliant' he continued. 'She's tired but it's superb. I'll have a drink later on and celebrate.' Asked about the name he said, 'It's David's and Victoria's choice, so obviously it's what they wanted. It is unusual. It's the same as Brooklyn. But I know, if he turns out half as good as Brooklyn, he'll be wonderful. The name's quite catching.'

The nation was perplexed. Not only could no one work out

why the name was chosen, but also the whole country had been expecting a girl. There had been reports, a couple of months previously, that Brooklyn had blurted out in a shop, 'I'm going to have a little sister called Paris,' but if he did, he had either misunderstood or he had become as adept at media manipulation as his parents. As for the name, there was one hint that it might have been inspired by David's love of garage music. One particular favourite group was So Solid Crew, especially MC Romeo.

'Big up, Becks,' said the singer himself. 'It's a great name. But then again, I am biased.'

David was unable to stay long: the next day he had to go back up north to resume training. But Victoria's mother was on hand to look after her daughter. Two days after the birth, she and Brooklyn went to the hospital bearing several bags of designer wear for newborns – and a silver football. They had been to Bobbit and Doodles, which specialised in very expensive clothing for children. 'He has been bought some designer babywear, jeans, sweatshirts, teddies and other bits and pieces,' said a source at the shop.

David lost no time in having his Adidas red boots embossed with the name. 'Romeo' was stitched on the tongue just above Brooklyn, just in time for the Premiership match against Middlesbrough, and flown to Manchester from Germany. 'We had a race against time to get them to Old Trafford before kick-off, but we knew what it meant to David,' said an Adidas spokesman.

Three days later, David escorted Victoria from the hospital, using the usual procedure, involving a couple of cars and the back entrance. 'They were fine and seemed very proud of the baby,' said personnel services manager Chris Jones. 'They were all very happy, they went away very happy.'

It was a timely moment to launch the range of Marks & Spencer's children's wear designed by the proud father. The DB07 range, for which David was paid £2 million – he was contracted to produce five collections in all – featured sporty T-shirts, wide-leg tracksuit trousers and zip-up jackets, and he was clearly delighted with his new role. 'When Marks & Spencer offered me the opportunity to actively assist in the design of clothing for youngsters, I was delighted,' he said. 'I want to create the kind of clothes that I would have wanted to wear when I was younger. Having Brooklyn helped me a lot. I like buying him outfits that I think look good on him and that's the style I wanted to go for with these clothes. The range includes two larger tops I'm sure Victoria will want to wear.'

Towards the end of September, David achieved yet another ambition: to captain United in the Champions League against Bayer Leverkusen. It was only to be a one-off as Roy Keane was only temporarily away and David had often said he knew he'd never get the position while Keane was there, but it was a testament to the faith that Sir Alex had in him and it made subsequent events all the sadder. It also marked David's tenth year with the club.

'I have to admit, I never had David down as a captain,' said Fergie. 'But the thing that impressed me was how well he responded to being made captain of England, because I honestly never saw him as a leader of that nature. He was always a quiet lad in the dressing room with us. But the way he fitted into the role of leading England has been fantastic and he's improved as a player through that. That's why I appointed him captain while Roy is out. David rarely misses a game for us and you don't want to be changing the captain every two or three games because of injury. Back when he started, he was just skin and bones, but you could tell he had a special talent and it was just a question of him filling out.'

But there was an ominous hint of what was to come. 'I think David's best when he's concentrating on his football with us,' Ferguson continued. 'He has a high profile and it's difficult to say how young people handle that. All I can say on the matter is that David's incredible in the way he handles it all.' Sir Alex may have been paying tribute to David's ability to cope with his high profile, but it looked like he didn't like it.

David remained blithely unaware of the matter and promptly made an appearance in the middle of Manchester wearing something that looked like an Alice band in his hair, but which was actually called a Flexicomb. Onlookers actually stopped and stared. 'It's not the sort of hairdo you'd expect to see on a top footballer,' said one. 'I bet he'll get a lot of stick about it in the Manchester United dressing room.'

It wasn't just the Mancunian shoppers who commented on

the new style – yet again, it made almost all the papers. As ever, David shrugged it off.

In early October, David was invited to a reception at 10 Downing Street, along with the rest of the England team. Just for once David was not the centre of attention: all eyes were on Nancy Dell'Olio, who had arrived in a striking red outfit. Sven had recently been in the news himself because of a dalliance with Ulrika Jonsson and Nancy was quite pointedly showing the world what Sven saw in her.

In November, Victoria was again at the centre of a security scare when four men and a woman were arrested for conspiracy to snatch her. It was the second time she had been the subject of a kidnap attempt, this time thought to be for a £5-million ransom. It later emerged that the threat was not quite as serious as it first appeared, but at the time David and Victoria were horrified.

'I'm incredibly grateful,' said Victoria after the arrest. 'It's scared the life out of me. I'm stunned by what has happened today. It's terrifying to think that someone would want to do that to you and your children. I'm in absolute and total shock. We have good security. We are very aware of the risks. But, if people want to do this to my family, how can you be 100 per cent sure you'll prevent it? If someone is that mad and that sick, what can you do? I don't think this will sink in for a while. I'm just so shocked.'

David was deeply shocked. 'The first role of a father and husband is to keep his family safe,' he said, before ordering increased security at his home. More CCTV cameras were fitted at the Hertfordshire mansion and more security men and equipment were installed. Sir Alex reacted with kindness, and offered David time off to spend with his family, although in the event David decided to take his mind off his worries by training. Indeed, he felt it would be giving into the would-be attackers if he didn't play.

David's friend Gary Neville vowed support for the player. 'It's not the first time, nor will it be the last, that this type of thing has happened,' he said. 'It's because of who he is. We have rallied around him and supported him. He should not have to deal with the things that he does. It's just the world we live in and it's not right.'

David showed up at training and was deemed ready to play in the Worthington Cup against Leicester – if, that is, Sir Alex picked him. 'David will be considered, but I will make a final decision about that tomorrow,' said Fergie. 'Knowing David, he will want to play – he always does. He likes training and he likes playing football. Obviously, if it was really necessary for him, of course we would have given him time off. But the thing is under control. The police have acted with great alacrity. They have done their job well. There is no threat to David so therefore it is business as usual.'

David did play and ended up slamming home a late penalty, with United winning 2–0. Matters calmed down slightly after that, although the family remained more security-conscious than ever, even ordering a bulletproof car.

Even so, it had been an unpleasant shock and so where

better to unwind than a health resort? For once this was not a case of David discovering his feminine side – rather, it was Sven-Göran Eriksson's idea. The whole team was taken to Champney's Health Resort in Hertfordshire for a three-day rest, combining therapy with training. Sven was his usual laid-back self about the whole thing. 'When you're in charge of a national team, you very seldom see your players,' he said. 'It's more difficult to have an atmosphere and spirit like a club where you see them every morning. So hopefully the players will like this break and become closer to each other. I think me being close to the players is good – although, as in life, I don't like just sitting with them chatting about nothing. But, if I have something to tell them, I'll do that.'

David had to miss the first day but bonded happily with the rest of the team on the break. And having met Tony Blair at Number 10, he was now moving in still more exalted circles when he went to Buckingham Palace to see the Queen. A special reception was held for the England football squad and the Football Association, and it emerged that even the monarch had heard about the kidnap scare.

'She raised the subject of security and if anyone's going to know about that, it's the Queen,' said Beckham. 'We spoke about increased security and how it would change our lives. It will definitely change things but it's just something that has to be done. She does know about football but spoke about security. It's something on my mind and obviously something the Queen lives with every day.'

David took Victoria and the boys to Barbados for a much-needed break, but on his return he was appalled to find untrue rumours about his private life were in circulation on the Internet, originating from the website Popbitch. After the trauma of the last month, he had quite clearly had enough and, after announcing there was absolutely no truth in the gossip, contacted his lawyers to threaten legal action. It did the trick. 'There was stuff on the website last week that was untrue and libellous about David,' snapped his spokesperson. 'We sent a legal letter telling them to remove it. They have done that. If anyone repeats it, they will be sued.'

After all the drama of the last months, David needed some light relief and got it by having Romeo's name tattooed on his back, while joking that there was still room for a few more. Going on BBC1's *Breakfast with Frost* alongside Sven-Göran Eriksson, David also tackled the thorny subject of his hair. He styled it himself, he revealed, saying, 'It's whatever I feel like when I wake up in the morning.' And did his mother ever comment? 'She does,' said David. 'She tells me if I look silly at times, but thankfully it's not that often – well, in my eyes, it's not that often.'

And, given security scares and Internet rumours – to say nothing of the furore surrounding Sven's private life – was the price of fame getting too high to pay? 'I think something needs to be done about certain things but, you know, it's part and parcel of being a footballer and being a manager these days,' David replied. 'It's unfortunate that your private life comes into the game because, at the end of the day, all I've wanted to do is to play football all my life. The other thing has to come with it, the fame and everything else, but I'm a footballer. It's hard to come to terms with certain things, but, you know, you can cope with it.' Of course, it helped that Victoria was also so famous. Just as they did in the earliest days of their relationship, the couple relied on each other to help them rise above all the madness.

David's tattooist, Louis Molloy, elaborated on his latest artwork. 'Everybody's seen the angel figure on his back – now I've put wings on it,' he revealed. 'Where the angel's head is bowed, we've put a halo above it. Then we've put Romeo's name above the halo. The whole thing took about two hours and he's very pleased with it. Becks told me he fancied having as many as five kids, so it looks like I'm going to be busy.'

As Christmas approached, the Beckhams had Romeo baptised and prepared to face a gruelling year ahead. Quite how gruelling it was going to be was still not clear. David's profile was set to rise higher still, with him now famous in just about every country in the world outside the States. He and Victoria now could not so much as change their hairstyle without commanding blanket coverage and, given that both were prone to doing just that at the drop of a hat, they were to become more exposed than ever. If anything, the couple seemed to have stepped into the gap left by Princess Diana. They were young, beautiful, vibrant, rich – and, to cap it all, they were in love.

But one person who, despite his kindness over the kidnap scare, was getting increasingly sick of the circus surrounding Beckham was Sir Alex Ferguson. He had seen David grow from a short, shy boy from south London to a global icon, whose fame seemed sometimes to eclipse his football. Worse still, he had become interested in fashion and, worse even than that, he often seemed in thrall to his wife. But worst of all was something Sir Alex really could not tolerate. David was now so famous he was actually bigger than Manchester United. And, in Sir Alex's eyes, no one gets bigger than the club.

CHAPTER 12

MANCHESTER 2003

A t the start of the new year, it seemed nothing could mar David's golden existence. Victoria and the children were at the centre of his life, he was at the peak of his powers as a footballer and he was, to put it bluntly, rolling in it. At £3.5 million a year from United, he was one of the best-paid footballers in the country and his sponsorship deals now included Police sunglasses, Brylcreem, Marks & Spencer, Vodafone, Adidas, Pepsi and Rage Software. He had three houses, each one a mansion, a vast car collection and everything in the world to look forward to. What could possibly go wrong?

Very ironically, David kicked off 2003 by starring in an advertisement for Pepsi that also featured Real Madrid's goalkeeper, Casillas. The two could have had no idea that just six months on they would be playing for the same team – indeed, they were cast opposite each other as the good guy and the villain in the ad, based on the classic *Gunfight at the OK*

Corral. It showed David riding into town with four compadres: his United teammates Gary Neville, Juan Sebastian Veran, Ryan Giggs and Ole Gunnar Solskjaer. David walks into the bar, demands a Pepsi – and Casillas drinks it. David orders him outside. The two engage in a penalty shootout. The end.

David certainly looked the part even if he didn't quite sound it – that voice again – prompting speculation that an acting career might be on the cards. And, again, he was being hailed as a thoroughly modern icon for our times. This time round it was a piece of serious academic research: a study called 'One David Beckham: Celebrity, Masculinity and the Soccerati' by Dr Andrew Parker of Warwick University and Professor Ellis Cashmore of Staffordshire University. The work was done for a conference examining the growing phenomenon of sports stars as celebrities and it certainly didn't hold back, claiming that David was the most influential man in England by transforming male attitudes towards love, babies, sex, laddism and homosexuality.

'David Beckham is a hugely important figure in culture and probably now the most influential male figure for anyone in Britain aged five to 60,' said Dr Parker. 'By defying expectations in areas such as what clothes men are allowed to wear, he has helped create a complex new concept of masculinity. That has already begun to change male behaviour and has the potential to encourage a whole generation of men who admire him to act more like him.'

It was heady stuff and there was a good deal more to come. 'He is "new man" (nurturer, compassionate partner, paternally adept) and "new lad/dad lad" (soccer hero, fashionable footballer, conspicuous consumer), while still demonstrating the vestiges of "old industrial man" (loyal, dedicated, stoic, bread-winning),' they wrote. 'Despite his high profile and the ridicule he risks, Beckham stands resolute: bucking the "macho" trend, setting his own agenda, showing support for his wife, playing the perfect father, remaining every mother's favourite – while at the same time, on the field, displaying the spirit and patriotism of a national ambassador.'

Could it get any better? Yes. David was praised for his love of Victoria, fashion and ballet, pretty much in that order, and subverting every male stereotype you can think of. 'He has broken so many strict traditional working-class masculine codes of behaviour that he has the potential to influence lots of boys and young men to do the same – for example, accepting homosexuality as a part of life,' said Dr Parker. 'We hope a spin-off will be to make the world a better, more tolerant place. Although Beckham is still "one of the lads" because he's a footballer, we never see him out drinking with the lads because he prioritises quality time with his family, which is highly unusual in the world of football. In terms of the gender order, Beckham is a law unto himself.'

Was this the straw that finally broke Sir Alex's back? To see David praised for the very qualities that he had grave misgivings about? To hear that David, the young boy he had sent to Preston to get him toughened up, was now the most influential man in Britain?

And, if all that were not enough, David insisted on putting his caring side on display yet again when Wayne Rooney, aged 17, became the youngest England player in history. David, of course, was going to be there for him. 'I used to go to Alan Shearer if I had a problem and Wayne can come to me if he needs any advice,' said the soft-spoken star. 'He's a quiet lad and, if he wants to talk to me, he only need ask. I wouldn't change a single thing from my past, even though I've had many ups and downs. I've stayed balanced through the good times, got through the bad times and became a better person for it.' It wasn't the sort of thing Roy Keane came up with. Is it any wonder Sir Alex felt a pang of downright despair?

Whatever the state of the tough old Glaswegian's feelings, it was less than a week after all this that a football boot flew through the air and connected with David's forehead. From that moment on, there was no going back.

The signs had been there from the very beginning and for some time now they had been flashing as brightly as the light on top of a police car. When Victoria's autobiography, *Learning To Fly*, had been published in 2001, she described Sir Alex as 'vindictive', said he never said more than 'hello' to her and revealed he 'went berserk' when David asked him for an additional two days off for his honeymoon. However, just as David had always said, she revealed that, despite all this, she'd always encouraged him to stay on at United. When it was finally time to go, the decision was not hers – nor even David's. It was down to Sir Alex.

CHAPTER 13

HOLA, MADRID!

The end of Beckham's career at Manchester United, when it came, was brutal. He was their most fêted star, and possibly the most famous footballer ever to emerge from Old Trafford, but events had moved too far. When a star footballer and his manager can no longer work together, something must give, and so it was in the summer of 2003, when the Beckhams were in Los Angeles to present an MTV award, part of their 'World Tour', that they learned of the sea change in their lives. On 10 June, David's agent, Tony Stephens, told him to look at the Man United website. What he saw was breathtaking in its abruptness:

Manchester United have released the following statement regarding David Beckham and Barcelona: 'Manchester

United confirms that club officials have met Joan Laporta, the leading candidate for the presidency of Barcelona. These meetings have resulted in an offer being made for the transfer for David Beckham to Barcelona. This offer is subject to a number of conditions and critically to Mr Laporta being elected president on Sunday 15 June and Barcelona subsequently reaching agreement with David Beckham on his personal contract. Manchester United confirms that in the event that all of the conditions are fulfilled, then the offer would be acceptable.'

This was no way to treat your talent. 'David is very disappointed and surprised to learn of this statement and feels that he has been used as a political pawn in the Barcelona presidential elections,' said a spokesman for his management company, SFX. 'David's advisors have no plans to meet Mr Laporta or his representatives.' Nor was David's father, Ted, particularly pleased. 'I shall tell him not to go there,' he said. 'I don't want him to go just because a certain person wants him to go.' But alas, when that certain person was Sir Alex Ferguson, Becks had no choice.

The writing had been on the wall for months, if not years though, making such an outcome inevitable. Fergie had frequently and publicly criticised David's celebrity lifestyle, but it was in February 2003 that matters really got out of hand. United lost 2–0 at home to Arsenal, after which Fergie, angry at the team's performance, visited the players' dressing room and kicked a boot; to everyone's horror, it flew in David's direction and struck him in the face and, according to some reports, left him needing stitches. It marked a point of no return: Sir Alex initially described it as a 'freakish accident', while David's injuries were highlighted by the media. There was no way back from there.

In making the announcement about Barcelona, Fergie's actions had almost certainly been made to open a bidding war, and so it proved. Real Madrid was known to be interested in Becks, but to date had offered only £15 million: that sum was soon to be massively increased. And so, as David and Victoria moved on to the Far East, wheels were set in motion. Real Madrid fixers Pedro López and José Ángel Sánchez arranged a meeting with United's chief executive Peter Kenyon and managing director Peter Gill in Sardinia: shortly afterwards, on 17 June, an announcement was made. Becks was moving to Real Madrid in a deal worth £25 million to United and £30 million to Beckham himself, sums so staggering that they were in themselves now a sign of the fact that he was far more than merely a footballer, but one of the world's global icons. The contract was set for four years, during which time he would be earning £120,000 a week.

David himself displayed a great deal of graciousness. 'I would like to publicly thank Sir Alex Ferguson for making me the player I am today,' he said. 'I will always hold precious memories of my time at Manchester United and Old Trafford, as well as the players, who I regard as part of my family, and the brilliant fans who have given me so much support over the years.'

In victory, Sir Alex could also afford to be magnanimous, issuing a statement of congratulations and best wishes for the future. There were mutters from quite a few commentators – and Ted Beckham – that David had been treated shabbily, but the die was now cast. Victoria's parents took a different line from Ted: Tony Adams went on the radio to talk about the advantages of having the children brought up in an international climate (something his daughter was going to take some time to come to accept), adding, when asked about Victoria's relationship with Sir Alex, 'Can I use the famous "no comment"?'

And so the Beckhams began to plan their move. For a start, some of David's car collection – an armour-plated Mercedes ML500, a Ferrari 550 Maranello and an Aston Martin DB7 – were to be shipped to the Spanish capital, while the others remained behind at Beckingham Palace. A brief holiday in the South of France followed, before David embarked on a tour of Asia with his new club. Victoria, in what was to set the tone of the early days in Madrid, stayed behind in England for a meeting with the Spice Girls' Svengali Simon Fuller in an attempt to restart her career, this time round by promoting 'Brand Beckham'.

The family moved to Madrid at the end of the summer, initially staying in hotels while they began to search for a house. David gave happy interviews, explaining that he would miss family and friends as well as 'pie and mash and jellied eels', but saying that he was looking forward to his new life. However, in retrospect, it is clear that for possibly the first time in their marriage, he and Victoria had either failed to think through the full implications of the move, or had thought, erroneously, that each had reached an accommodation with the other. Whatever the case, David was asked if Victoria would be accompanying him to Madrid: 'That's what we have to do,' he said. 'We have to fully commit ourselves to Spain and to Real Madrid, and that's what we're doing.'

He went on to explain that Victoria, as she always had, would travel to the UK and the States in pursuit of her own career, but he was firmly of the impression that the entire family would be moving with him. This is not, however, what happened.

But back then, in the late summer of 2003, all was sweetness and light. David's first appearance with his new team was judged to be a great success, while his new teammates were exposed for the first time to the full force of the media whirlwind that was Brand Beckham. The club's Hongta Sports press room was too small to hold the assortment of international journalists covering the team's first public statement with Beckham in their midst: David professed himself to be happy and beginning to learn a few words of Spanish – a language in which he has yet, it must be said, to show any proficiency whatsoever to this day.

As the Beckhams began to settle into their new life in Madrid, there were increasingly feverish reports about house hunting, with speculation that the couple were to buy a 12-bedroom mansion named La Victoria. Certainly the Beckham property portfolio was growing: that summer they also bought a sumptuous holiday home in the South of France, although at the time of writing, they have yet to spend a night there (some reports have it that Victoria won't stay there as it's rumoured to be haunted).

But in reality the couple were nowhere near buying a house in Madrid. Indeed, it was becoming increasingly obvious that Victoria didn't want to be there at all. She continued to live in Beckingham Palace, complaining privately that she didn't like the Spanish way of life. Jackie, her mother, unwisely supported her daughter in this path. David and Victoria had always spent a great deal of time apart, she told reporters who were becoming increasingly curious about the real state of affairs: this was no different to when David was at Man United.

Except, of course, it was very different indeed. David was by now living in a foreign country with a language he didn't understand, new teammates, who were welcoming and friendly, but nonetheless, acquaintances rather than friends, with no home of his own to stay in and only the comforts of a hotel. Nor did it ring any warning bells with anyone – except, perhaps, Jackie – when an attractive young woman called Rebecca Loos was assigned to look after him: Jackie reportedly warned Victoria that the only women around David should be gay. Victoria, in turn, laughed this off: Rebecca was, in fact gay, she said, an answer that was only half-right, for Rebecca was actually bisexual. It had all the makings of a crisis to come.

That all was not quite going to plan was illustrated by the fact that for the first time ever, articles began to appear in the press to the effect that there were problems in the marriage.

There was even speculation, though this was to prove wide of the mark, that they would divorce. Reports filtered out of screaming rows on the phone, with Victoria apparently telling David that she would leave him if he didn't return to England. The couple themselves didn't comment publicly: rather, they put on a great show of togetherness, one night visiting one of Madrid's swankiest restaurants before getting their driver to give them a tour of the city. But still the rumours went on.

In October, there was another upset when David was pictured at a Madrid nightclub, without Victoria, but with a group of other people, including Rebecca Loos. Shortly afterwards, Rebecca was quietly moved to another role. David himself then parted company with SFX management, amid frenzied speculation that he was to cut down on his promotional work, which was by now earning him about £24 million a year. A statement was released: 'His contract [with SFX] was due for renewal and he has decided with Euro 2004 and a busy year ahead at Madrid he will be focusing entirely on football and not taking on any new commercial activity in the short term, except as part of his club commitments. He will continue to work with his current sponsors.'

And still the stories about marital rows continued, so much so that Becks was finally provoked into speaking out. 'I'm fed up,' he said in November 2003. 'I love my wife; she loves me – there have never been any problems. My wife is very committed to her husband and children and people should stop making up silly stories. I keep commenting on it, when I shouldn't have to. I'm fed up with commenting on it.'

There was a let-up, of sorts, later in the month when David went to Buckingham Palace to receive his OBE. This was the kind of occasion at which David and Victoria excel: they arrived with the children in a silver Bentley, followed by a second Bentley carrying David's grandparents, who had been invited to watch the investiture. David was in morning dress, with Victoria looking exceedingly stylish in black: it was 'the best honour' he'd ever received, he said, adding, 'It's great to receive an award for playing football, for something I love doing. It's not just for me but for Manchester United, England, all of my teammates and my family.' Mindful of the rumours circling the couple, he also took the opportunity to express his feelings for his wife. 'I love her a lot,' he said. 'She's my wife, she's going to be with me whatever happens.' With that the party adjourned for lunch.

The year wound to a close. The Beckham extravagance was as in evidence as ever: shortly before Christmas, Victoria made the news when it emerged that she'd managed to spend $42,500 in the course of an afternoon. David seemed determined to keep the marriage on track: Victoria's present that year was a $1.7 million yacht and a $238,000 Bentley. 'Their marriage has been through the mill and David is desperate to keep the family together,' said a friend. 'Buying Victoria the boat means they can get together right away from pressures and relax. He's been looking for one for ages but only decided a few weeks ago.'

It was a quiet enough start to begin with in 2004: indeed

matters seemed to be calming down. Reports of rows between the couple were becoming less frequent; they seemed to have found a modus operandi, at least for the time being. But then in April came the event that was to blow the domestic set-up out of the water, so much so that there were real fears the marriage wouldn't survive. This was, of course, the allegation by Rebecca Loos that she had had a brief fling with David, a story that changed his image completely overnight. Until then, despite the fact that the marriage was clearly going through a stormy patch, David still maintained his image as the completely loyal husband and father, a new man as at home changing nappies as he was on the football pitch. But while no one has ever impugned his abilities as a father, the public perception of him went straight out the window. His reputation has not fully recovered, even to this day.

The story, when it appeared, came as a complete shock. The *News of the World* had been courting Loos for some time and had got her to send some sexually explicit text messages to David's mobile number: it appears he responded enthusiastically and at once. And so, one Sunday in April, a staggered world woke up to the fact that David Beckham, the world's best husband and father, had done the unthinkable when Victoria wasn't around several months previously and had had an affair.

It is testament to his enormous popularity and worldwide appeal that this story dominated certain sections of the news agenda, both at home and abroad. No one could really believe it. That David Beckham, who had pretty much broken the mould where footballers are concerned, could have turned out to have feet of clay after all was almost too much to bear.

The Beckhams were in Courcheval, in the South of France, when the story broke and, initially, tried to dampen speculation about the state of their marriage by horsing around in the snow. 'We have been through a lot worse than this and we're definitely going to get through it,' Victoria informed the hordes of reporters who had suddenly descended on the resort. It was 'ludicrous', said an incandescent David, who appeared barely able to contain himself about the whole episode.

But matters very quickly got worse. For a start, a second woman, the model Sarah Marbeck, came forward to claim that she, too, had had an affair with Beckham. Rebecca Loos, meanwhile, who seemed to be revelling in her sudden notoriety, publicly announced that she knew intimate physical details about David and would be perfectly prepared to reveal them should the couple try to take her to court. She followed that up by appearing on Sky television, where she proceeded to give a graphic account of the affair, despite the best efforts of the Beckham legal team to put a stop to the proceedings.

Victoria, commendably, rose above it all: 'I will not let that tart ruin my marriage,' she said. Support came from an unlikely quarter: the Hollywood superstar Uma Thurman, who had herself recently parted from her husband, commented, 'It sounds pretty low. I don't know the facts, though – I wasn't there. I'm not sure whether she's trash or a tramp. I'd say tramp, though. She can't get enough PR.'

In May it was announced that David was to become the first-ever sportsman to appear on the cover of the American magazine *Vanity Fair*. At around the same time, he very publicly bought Victoria a £1 million pink diamond ring for her birthday, although on the day itself, she was at home in Britain with the boys. By now, however, she had clearly realised that if she didn't eventually follow her husband to Madrid, their marriage was going to be in serious trouble and so, that month, it was finally announced that the entire family would be moving to Spain.

Both Beckhams were keen to clarify their feelings about the move: 'I have a long-term commitment to Real and to my life in Spain,' said David. 'I've been there for one season and it feels like the job is not done yet. The support that I have received from the fans has been amazing and I would like to see them repaid with success. Victoria shares my vision of our life together.'

She was only too keen to agree. 'The time is now right for the children to move to Madrid and we are all looking forward to it enormously,' she said. 'It is a fantastic city with wonderful people and David and I are looking forward to strengthening our links with both. We are all very excited.'

And the depth of David's fury over the whole episode was clear: the Football Association had agreed that Becks and Sven-Göran Eriksson would talk to Sky as part of a deal to screen two friendly games against Iceland and Japan: such was David's anger at the fact that the channel had allowed Rebecca Loos airtime that he refused point-blank to cooperate.

Finally, Victoria was also ready to speak out. She gave an

exclusive to *Marie Claire* magazine, in which she point-blank refuted suggestions that she was only staying with David because together they made such a bankable pair. 'I couldn't live a lie and it would be unfair to our children,' she said. 'We are working on things together, but our marriage is absolutely not a business arrangement. Could you for all the money in the world? I couldn't.'

Nor was David prepared to let it rest. Sporting a new, shorn haircut, he cut into an interview with Sky reporters – tensions there had eased – to make an announcement about what the previous weeks had been like. Asked how the team's training at the pre-Euro 2004 retreat in Sardinia was going, he said, 'Sorry, before I answer that question, can I just say something I want to say. As England captain I know I need to talk to the fans, and I understand the sports side is different to the news side and I think the way the news side have treated me in the last few months has been a disgrace.

'I've been called a bad father, I've been called a bad husband and my wife has been called a bad mother. Things always hurt that are said about my family, and for people to call my wife a bad mother is unbelievable. I'm a strong person, I'm a strong family man, I'm a strong husband and a strong father.' But at least the football was going well. 'I have enjoyed this season, whatever has gone on and whatever rumours there were about me moving back to England,' David continued. 'Those rumours were never started by me. I was always happy at Real and wanted to stay. The things that have always been said about me have never affected my football – that's the way it will always be.'

Of course, he had suffered some pretty appalling publicity in the past, but the difference was that before it had always been about his professional life. This was the first time he had ever been criticised on a personal basis and it hurt. Nor was it just his relationship with Victoria that was under scrutiny: the in-laws had been dragged in on the act, too. Victoria had always been very close to her parents, and so, given the allegations of her husband's infidelity, perhaps it was unsurprising that relations between David and his parents-in-law were said to have become a little strained. Victoria's mother decided to step in. 'I know that I've got the happiest daughter and son-in-law,' she said. 'There is absolutely nothing wrong with their relationship. They are as happy as they've ever been.'

Turning to her own relationship with David, she continued, 'David and I are really, really close. Why in the world would I not talk to him? He hasn't done anything to make me not talk to him.'

But not everyone agreed. By then, David had become such a global icon that it was a huge shock when a portrait of him, which featured in a photographic exhibition of great footballers, was defaced with the words, 'You losers'. It was 'enormously irritating', said David Grob, the show's curator, and slightly alarming for Beckham, too. The sheen was gone from his public image: to many, the qualities that had entirely set him apart from the other footballers on the field were now being questioned.

Now he was truly discovering the truth of the maxim, 'it never rains but it pours'. For a man who had seen everything he touched turn to gold for the best part of a decade, the headlines he was garnering just seemed to get worse and worse. There was constant speculation about the state of the marriage, and breaks with Victoria in Morocco and at Elton John's villa in the South of France did nothing to quell the rumours. Nor was life much better on the pitch: he missed two penalties in Euro 2004, one as England lost to France in the opening games and another in the quarterfinal penalty shoot-out defeat against Portugal. This led to even more bad headlines – and of course, with so much pressure on his personal life, his professional side was bound to suffer, too.

Some good did come out of this, however: it made the couple decide that from now on they really were going to be together and Victoria and the children made the final move. Talking to BBC's *Match of the Day*, David acknowledged that he had been under a great deal of stress. 'A lot of things were said about me last season that were not true,' he said. 'Looking back on it, I can see that maybe I was taking what was happening on and off the pitch with me onto the pitch in Portugal and that my performances may have suffered slightly. We are together as a family in Madrid now and that is wonderful. They were actually out here more last season than some people thought but we had trouble finding the right school for Brooklyn. Now we have got a school for him and a playgroup for Romeo, while Victoria is working from Madrid.'

It was not – by a long shot – to be the end of the rumours and speculation, but it was a start. More than anything else, despite having an even more torrid time of it than the two were used to, David and Victoria had at least shown the world their determination to stay together and keep their relationship strong. There was further proof of this in late August when it was announced that Victoria was expecting the couple's third child: 'This is fantastic news,' they said in a joint statement. 'We are both absolutely delighted. We are planning to have the baby in Spain.'

News of the pregnancy had clearly been a great boost to the couple, and with the family together now in Madrid, it might have been thought that the feverish speculation swirling around them would die down. But this was not to be: the two had created such a massive global persona – Brand Beckham – that they were simply unable to calm the resulting furore. And so, hardly had it been announced that Victoria was expecting a boy than reports of disagreements surfaced once more.

And they were more vicious than ever. Newspapers printed stories of alleged rows and disharmony, which must have been most distressing for the Beckhams to read.

Matters were not exactly helped when the couple pulled up in a car at a Madrid traffic light and saw, in the adjacent vehicle, one Rebecca Loos. Wisely they ignored her and drove on. Rebecca herself, who had been milking her brief fling for all it was worth, professed surprise and hurt, although what more she might have expected from the chance meeting is difficult to say. 'I saw him and then I just looked away,' she said. 'When I looked at him it was like he was nobody. I'd love to talk to Victoria but she wouldn't have it. I don't think she would like to hear what I have to say anyway.'

David's mood was not improved when it was announced that Marks & Spencer was not going to renew the contract for his clothing range: the items had not sold well, which was hardly surprising given that Rebecca Loos now seemed intent on turning up like the bad fairy at every available feast. Victoria was 'in denial' over the affair, she claimed, as well she might be. It seemed as sensible a survival strategy as any.

But the tap of gossip was now running at full strength. First it was announced that Rebecca Loos was to appear in a documentary about Becks, and then yet another alleged lover, Danielle Heath, crawled out of the woodwork. Danielle had been, of all things, the Beckhams' tanning assistant, and now she too claimed to have been fooling around with David, although matters stopped short of a full-blown fling. The Beckhams lashed out in return, issuing a joint statement to the press. 'We are sick and tired of people trying to make money at the expense of our family,' it read. 'It is even more distressing when we are expecting our third child soon. These allegations are completely and totally untrue and the matter is in the hands of our lawyer.'

As 2004 drew to a close, Elton John popped up to talk about the Beckhams, although this time round he was being a little indiscreet. It was no secret that the family had been having a rough time of it, but quite how rough was now laid open for all to see. The problems began, he explained, when David moved to Madrid and Victoria stayed put to concentrate on her career. 'I think they should have gone together as a family,' he said. 'I think he missed her and the boys terribly. What's happened now is that she's so disillusioned with all that career stuff that she's quite happy to be there. But at that time she wasn't and was trying to prove something. But you learn from your mistakes. I think it's affected him mentally and it affected his form. And basically the worm turned ... they were the darlings of the press, and then the press turned.'

Nor, according to Elton, did they deal with the Loos situation, as they should have done. 'They should have just put a statement out saying something like: "Every marriage has its ups and downs and we're just going through a down phase at the moment",' he said. 'But they just denied it and kept denying it, and there were obviously problems ... which now they seem to have sorted out.' Of course, Sir Elton was speaking from a gay perspective, which is generally more accepting of flings within long-term relationships. He might not have understood that accepting it was simply not an option for the wronged wife in this particular case.

There was further media furore when David and Victoria featured as Joseph and Mary in a nativity scene at Madame

Tussauds: indeed, soon afterwards it was attacked by a member of the public and the museum were forced to close it down. It was unsurprising that the scene had not gone down well with the public – Cardinal Cormac Murphy O'Connor, head of the Roman Catholic Church in England and Wales called it 'disrespectful', and he was right – but the Beckhams themselves were not to blame. Their image was everywhere and even they themselves had increasingly little control over how it was being used.

The couple seemed determined to finish what had been a very difficult year on a positive note, however. A few days before Christmas, Brooklyn and Romeo were christened in a ceremony at Beckingham Palace that was positively overflowing with celebrity guests. The children's godfather, Sir Elton, was in attendance, as was Elizabeth Hurley, conspicuously breaking the 'no-cleavage' rule. A chapel had been erected in the grounds for the occasion, while the service was conducted by Paul Colton, the Bishop of Cork, who had been the churchman to marry the pair. Elton sang, David gave a speech and the guests were sent away with a goody bag containing, among other things, a single diamond. It was a harmonious end to a very fractious year.

To begin with, at least, 2005 looked as if it was going to be rather calmer than the year that had preceded it. On 20 February, Victoria gave birth to the couple's third son, Cruz, in a planned Caesarian section at the Ruber International Hospital in Madrid. David radiated happiness as he divulged the news. 'I have two beautiful sons already and now I have another beautiful son called Cruz,' he said. 'He's gorgeous, healthy and his mum is very good. We're a very happy family. He's got Victoria's lips and nose.'

There was some comment when David missed Victoria's birthday in April, although in truth there was nothing more sinister behind it than that he was playing in a match 200 miles away. The calm, however, did not last long. It sometimes seemed that everyone with whom David and Victoria had dealings became aware of the cash value of the relationship and now it emerged that their former nanny, Abbie Gibson, was no different. She, too, provided an insight into the couple's relationship via the pages of a Sunday newspaper, and it was not a pretty sight. The pair had descended into screaming obscenities at one another in the early hours of the morning, according to Abbie, while Victoria, at the time still pregnant with Cruz, was terrified David was going to leave her.

This time, however, the Beckhams had had enough and they attempted to take out an injunction to stop the allegations being published. Although their first attempt failed, the two, irritated beyond endurance, went straight back to court. And this time it was hard not to feel at least a small amount of sympathy for them. For all that they'd spent years invading their own privacy, to have their own nanny turn on them was hard indeed. Victoria, straight to the point as always, called Abbie a 'two-faced cow'. 'Yeah, we have our arguments, of course we do – but all couples row, don't they? So at least it makes us bloody normal. To be honest, I'm more sad that this happened now, because me and David are really happy.'

Becks himself was equally livid. 'I'm being portrayed as some kind of uncaring monster and Victoria is meant to be the Wicked Witch of the West,' he snapped. 'I am sick of it. It's just people selling stories for money. I'm sick and tired of everybody having a go at us just for being a normal couple. We're happily married and are going to stay that way.'

The Abbie Gibson row, however, was still rumbling on. David and Victoria really were determined to stop their former nanny from spilling yet more beans, with the result that their own lawyers had to make the sensational announcement that a good deal of what she was saying was true. 'The fact a couple have arguments, and one of the couple might have said in the heat of the moment they wanted to split up, does not mean they are not happily married,' said Hugh Tomlinson, the Beckhams' lawyer, but of course all that came out of that was the fact that he had confirmed one of them – David – had threatened to leave the other.

It was turning pretty nasty. In response David issued a statement saying that he had always treated women with respect: Abbie came back with a really vicious remark detailing his various alleged affairs and behaviour towards Victoria. That Britain's erstwhile golden couple could have come to this continued to shock those around them: this was simply not what people were used to hearing about David Beckham, and no amount of chatting about eye creams could mend that.

CHAPTER 14

LA CALLING

Behind all the nonsense, it was business as usual. Having announced that she was giving up singing, Victoria was now pursuing a career in fashion, while David followed his dream of opening up a fleet of sports academies across the world. One academy was already open in London and now David was to be the partner in a similar one in Los Angeles, too. He joined Simon Fuller and Tim Leiweke, the president and chief executive of Anschutz Entertainment Group, to reveal the plans. 'I've opened one in London and I'm opening one in LA,' he said. 'It's about kids coming down, getting off the streets, having fun ...'

Asked if he might one day consider a full-time move to the United States, David was enthusiastic. 'Yeah, I think it's always a possibility,' he admitted. 'In my career, things have happened and situations have happened and I never, ever thought that I'd be playing anywhere apart from England. But I'm playing in Spain now, and there is an opportunity to come to America, and I am thinking about it, definitely.' It would probably be easier for Victoria to adapt to the States than it had been for her to get used to Spain, too.

While the couple were in LA, they were invited to the home of their new friend, Tom Cruise. And Becks' appeal appeared to be withstanding the nannygate revelations. In May he was wheeled out as one of the most high profile supporters for London to gain the Olympics in 2012, appearing alongside the then Prime Minister Tony Blair and Lord Coe, the bid chairman, at a presentation in Singapore. 'We back the bid because we believe it will inspire young people and give them the chance to see an Olympics in our own country,' said David, speaking alongside Victoria.

That summer, he was the subject of more scrutiny, but this time around the scrutiniser was none other than his father Ted, in the shape of a book. 'It's come together really well,' said Ted. 'I talk about everything. The book is all about the early days right the way up to Madrid. But there's no dirty stuff in it – I wouldn't do that. David didn't always know I was doing it, but I'm really chuffed with it. I've sent him a copy, but I haven't had a response yet because he's away now.'

In actual fact, David and Victoria were said to be none too pleased when they heard the news but, as so often, money seemed to have played a part. Ted was still working as a gas fitter when he wrote it and had spoken publicly about the cost of the plane fare when he went to see David play in Madrid, compared to what he'd had to pay to see his son play for Man United. He apparently received a six-figure advance for the tome – which actually turned out to be fairly innocuous – and perhaps thought that if everyone else was making so much money out of the Beckham image, why should he not do so as well? Victoria's parents actually worked as paid assistants to the famous couple. There was a good deal of speculation that Ted resented this and would have liked to be in that position, too.

In the event, a few eyebrows were raised when the book came out, not least because it appeared that Ted had exactly the same reservations about David's relationship with Victoria as Sir Alex. 'I can't pretend that we were totally thrilled that David was going out with a pop star,' he wrote. 'We weren't worried about Victoria, it was more the sort of lifestyle someone in her world has to lead ... going to clubs, staying out late, sleeping in in the mornings ... It is all the exact opposite of what a footballer's life should be. [But] even if we'd disapproved, it wouldn't have made any difference. David is as stubborn as I am and once he's made his mind up, that's it, he's going to go through with it.'

Whatever feelings the family might have had about Ted's book, however, were soon overshadowed by something of much greater concern. Little Romeo was taken into the hospital for the second time in two months after he was suffering from convulsions. Initially the child was treated at the Ruber International Clinic in Madrid before suffering a third fit, after which he was flown back to Britain for further tests. It was not announced at the time, but has subsequently emerged that Romeo has epilepsy.

A little more light relief came about after Victoria had a row with the 50-year-old Ana Obregon, a woman who had ostentatiously checked into the same hotel as David on his move to Madrid, and had subsequently tried her hardest to put it about that the two of them were an item. A clearly fed-up Victoria had had enough, as became apparent when she confronted Ana, clad in hot pants and shocking pink, in a health club. 'Why would he be interested in an old lady like you?' she snapped. 'Leave my husband alone. Go get some clothes on and act your age!'

But the mood was soured slightly at the end of the year when it emerged that the Beckhams had failed to invite Ted to Christmas celebrations in Beckingham Palace. They were said to be still upset about the book, with a source close to David saying, 'David was devastated when he found out his dad was writing the book. He can't understand why Ted never mentioned anything to him. Becks feels his dad has betrayed him.' Ted was feeling pretty wistful, too. 'Obviously I feel upset, but I'd rather not say anything,' he admitted. 'I don't know who they've invited – I haven't got a clue.'

David also chose to come clean about a particular problem he had – the fact that he suffers from OCD, or Obsessive Compulsive Disorder. Everything from clothes to cans of coke has to be in order, he said, even in hotel rooms. 'I have got this obsessive compulsive disorder where I have to have everything in a straight line or everything has to be in pairs,' he revealed. 'I'll put my Pepsi cans in the fridge' – it was noticeable that even here, when discussing his condition, David did not forget to mention his sponsor – 'and if there's one too many then I'll put it in another cupboard somewhere. I've got that problem. I'll go into a hotel room. Before I can relax I have to move all the leaflets and all the books and put them in a drawer. Everything has to be perfect. I would like to [get rid of it]. I've tried and I can't stop.'

This was a genuine ailment, and one which caused him to take part in any number of strange rituals. David revealed that he wore a new pair of football boots for each match, bought exactly 20 packets of SuperNoodles every time he went to the supermarket and would spend hours making sure the furniture was straight. Victoria confirmed her husband's problem. 'Everything has to match in the house,' she said. 'If there are three cans of Diet Pepsi, he'd throw one away because it's uneven.'

This was not, however, news to David's teammates at Man United, who used to tease him mercilessly. Paul Scholes, Nicky Butt, Ryan Giggs and Gary and Phil Neville would come into his hotel room and quite deliberately mess everything up. 'I thought they were just coming in for a chat,' Becks related. 'But then they'd go out and I'm thinking, Something's different here. And then all the magazines would be all wonky. They'd have been in my wardrobe and all my trousers and my shoes would be all over the place – it was a joke with them.'

His condition even applied to the number of tattoos he had, he said. 'Funnily enough, and I know it sounds weird, but I actually enjoy the pain,' he admitted. 'Victoria's not keen on my having many more, but they are addictive.'

What was to be David Beckham's last World Cup as England captain was now looming and in retrospect, it's fair to say he went out in style. The couple had been planning their pre-World Cup party for some time now, with invitations going out for the Full Length and Fabulous Ball on 21 May 2006. Robbie Williams and James Brown provided the music, while Gordon Ramsay was in charge of catering. The guest list included Tom Cruise, Liz Hurley, Sir Elton John, the Osbournes, Ewan McGregor, Kate Moss and Elle Macpherson. Sarah Ferguson, accompanied by her daughter Beatrice, was also one of the guests and annoyed Victoria by flirting, very ostentatiously, with David before moving on to the dancefloor.

With that the circus moved on to Frankfurt ahead of the World Cup. The German press wasn't about to take any prisoners: the tabloid *Bild* had a go at various members of the family, including Sandra – 'a smile like a peasant' – and Joanne. It caused a bit of an outcry in the papers back home: while David and Victoria had sought publicity, the thinking seemed to be that the rest of the family should be left alone.

David himself wasn't pleased, calling the person who wrote the piece, 'sad and unacceptable'. 'When it comes to my family that is one thing I won't accept and never will,' he said. 'I find it sad that one person drops to the level of criticising my family, but it is one sad person thinking what they can do to put me off my next game. I've had enough things said about me outside of my football career to not worry about something like this. I do find it sad but I've always had a great relationship with the German public – it's never been a problem.'

But he soon had more to worry about: the World Cup was turning out to be something of a damp squib, with a lacklustre England failing to shine, never more so than when they played Portugal in the quarterfinal and lost. Beckham had been forced to leave the pitch in the 52nd minute of the game: he had an Achilles injury that was to force him out of action for at least six weeks. England went on to lose on penalties. It was the end of an era and David knew it.

And so he took the decision to step down as England captain and did so with a good deal of grace, too. He read out a statement at England's final news conference in Germany: 'I feel the time is right to pass on the armband as we enter a new era under new coach Steve McClaren,' he said. 'On 15 November 2000, Peter Taylor gave me the greatest honour of my career in making me the captain of England, fulfilling my childhood dream.'

It was an exceedingly dignified way to step down, but it provoked shock in some quarters, not least from Sven-Göran Eriksson. 'He's been a very good captain and very proud to do the job,' he said. 'I was a bit surprised when he told me but you have to respect his decision. It is now Steve McClaren's job to decide on Beckham's successor. He has a lot of choices that are more than capable of doing the job – it is very much up to him.'

Shortly afterwards it emerged that David was to be dropped from the England squad by the new coach, Steve McClaren – something he clearly didn't expect. 'He [McClaren] called me when I was getting on a plane for 15 hours to America ... and he said there's going to be casualties along the way and unfortunately you're one of the casualties,' David later revealed. 'It surprised me, I must admit, and I am gutted 'cos playing for England was everything to me. I still hope that I'm going to play for England again – I don't want to retire from international football.' He added: 'If I was a betting man I wouldn't bet on me playing again, but who knows?'

Tom Cruise was another person who helped David in his hour of need. 'When I got to America, I phoned Tom,' said Becks. 'He's a great guy to be able to speak to because he is a very positive-minded person. It is good to have people around you at that point. He talked about everything I had done in the World Cup, about the goal I scored and the goals I set up. He said I was a great player, that I played for Real Madrid, I've got a healthy family and three boys and a wife who love me to bits. He's a great example of someone who stays positive through everything. And that's how I started to get over what had happened with the England news. I got over it that way, with friends around me.'

And David and Victoria continued to make Beckingham Palace ever more completely their own. Already they had installed a £120,000 imitation medieval castle, a £100,000 Wendy House and a £100,000 two-hole golf course, and now plans were afoot to build a £300,000 infinity maze to add to that. Planning permission had been sought for a maze consisting of two circles making the figure 'eight', symbolising eternity (and the eternal nature of the couple's love), covering about 11,250 square feet. It was to measure 150 by 75ft, while the two circles were similar to those at Hever Castle in Kent. Tony Adams, Victoria's father, was to oversee the work, which was to include four benches and a two statues in the centre, and the Beckhams themselves could not wait.

'The mazes will be Victoria's pride and joy,' said a friend. 'They'll be great fun for the family to play in – while symbolising how much they love each other. The twin joys of Victoria's life are satisfied by the maze – their love and their happiness for their three boys. But it's not just a serious gesture: Victoria can see the tongue-in-cheek side of the extravagance. It's not yet been decided who will be sculpted for the two busts, but don't rule out David and Victoria featuring. David and Victoria have always played up to their role as the King and Queen of Showbiz. From the idea of marrying on thrones to the term for their home as Beckingham Palace, they've always been amused by the regal ideas – this will add to it.'

With David's footballing career entering its autumn years, clearly the duo were now beginning to think more carefully about what the future held. Both liked the United States and it was becoming obvious that that was where the opportunities for each of them lay. There had been some speculation that they would stay on in Spain after David left Real Madrid, but it is difficult to understand the reasoning behind that – the States seemed a much more obvious choice. There were rumours that David had been in talks with Philip Anschutz about joining the New York Red Bulls, while Victoria was said to be keen to launch a fashion series on US TV.

'They have set their sights on becoming American idols,' said a source close to the couple. 'Both are determined to make their dreams come true over in the States. David gets on amazingly well with Anschutz – there is a real mutual respect. David has made no secret of his love for America and is keen to become the face of soccer over there once his time with Real Madrid is over.'

It was with that pragmatic thought in mind that Becks accepted a £128 million five-year deal to play for the American team LA Galaxy at the beginning of 2007. The move made various records, with David set to earn a staggering £500,000 a week, although he was adamant it was not the financial rewards that were to take him Stateside. 'It's the right time for us to do it,' he explained. 'I don't want to go out to America when I'm 34 years old with people turning round and saying, "Well, he's only going there to get the money."'

His decision was greeted very differently on either side of the pond. In Britain there was a great deal of harrumphing about early lost promise and how materialistic Beckham had become, while in the States there was widespread euphoria about attracting one of the biggest names in sport over to those shores. 'David Beckham will have a greater impact on

avid Beckham after the final whistle for Man U vs. Real Madrid in the UEFA
iampions League.

Top: Another goal for Beckham; this time against Finland.

Bottom: Becks receives the captain's armband from coach Peter Taylor.

op left: The evening after being named top sports star in the fashion stakes at the le Style Awards, 1999. David steps out with Posh Spice in the sarong that whipped e tabloids into a frenzy. Nowadays, Beckham's numerous hairstyle changes never il to make the front pages.

p right: The happy couple out walking their Rottweiler puppies.

ottom: Engaged!

Top left: Already the perfect family, Victoria, David and Brooklyn leave Victoria's mum's house to go to the airport. They flew to Ireland for their wedding.

Top right: And what a wedding it was! 14½ months in the planning, the union of Posh and Becks overshadowed even that of Prince Edward and Sophie Rhys-Jones..

Bottom left: The man who made fatherhood sexy. David shops with Brooklyn … again.

Bottom right: David's football boots – the name of the newly born 'Romeo' has been added above his brother's.

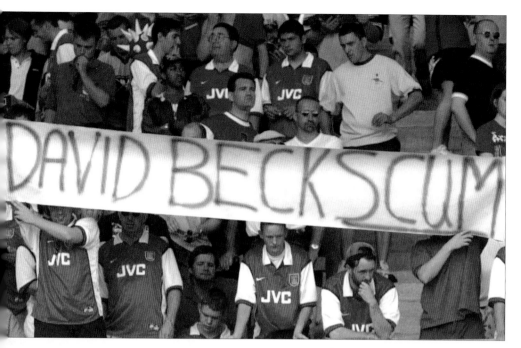

top: David Beckham has been adored – but he has also been despised. This picture shows the behaviour of some Arsenal fans during an Arsenal vs. Man United Charity Shield match.

bottom left: *That* red card – Becks is sent off by referee Kim Milton Nielson during the second round match between Argentina and England in the World Cup Finals, 1998.

bottom right: A dummy hanging as a representation of David Beckham. This was the work of south London football hooligans after the England vs. Argentina match in the 1998 World Cup.

With all the pressures of intensive media coverage on top of his football career, David needs all the relaxation he can get. *Top*: David is pictured on holiday in Marbella, kissing a pregnant Victoria. *Bottom*: The couple's huge mansion in the south of England, dubbed 'Beckingham Palace' by the press.

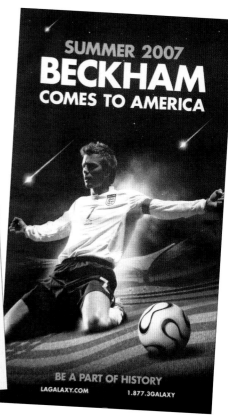

eckham-mania hits an excited America that couldn't quite believe he was on his way.
adame Tussauds even commissioned a special display *(top)* to welcome him.

Top left: David training with LA Galaxy.

Top right: David applauds AC Milan fans during their Champions League clash with his former club, Manchester United.

Bottom: Although he sadly missed the 2010 World Cup through injury, David travelled to South Africa as an ambassador and mentor for the team. He was also a key player in England's bid to host the 2018 World Cup and commands great respect from players, fans and managers worldwide.

soccer in America than any athlete has ever had on a brand globally,' said Timothy Leiweke, president of Anschutz Entertainment Group, which owns LA Galaxy.

Fabio Capello, the coach of Real Madrid, was certainly among those who were not impressed, declaring publicly that Beckham would not play for the team again. It was a very different scenario to that when David left Manchester United: although tensions between him and Sir Alex Ferguson had become insurmountable, both had had the grace to pay tribute to each other when David moved. Now, however, it was widely suspected that Capello was criticising his erstwhile star in order to shift attention from his own slightly ignominious performance. Meanwhile, Beckham was being forced to carry on for the final six months of his contract, meaning he couldn't join LA Galaxy until August.

Another American idol, Sylvester Stallone, was in no doubt as to the reception he would get. 'I am sure that in America David Beckham will be received as a superstar, no question about that,' he said. 'He has the looks, the whole thing, and he'll be welcomed with open arms. He will bring a tremendous amount of interest and supporters to the sport. Twenty per cent of America is Latino and they live for soccer. With Beckham there, it will really take off. *Escape To Victory* might as well have been made in Chinese. But the world's changing and I feel there will be a big revolution in America over football. I've not met Beckham, but I might put him in *Rambo* and chase him around the jungle for a couple of months!'

Certainly the US was jubilant and pushing out all the stops

to welcome their new hero. In January, shortly after the announcement that David Beckham was going to move was made, he became one of three stars – the others were Scarlett Johansson and Beyoncé Knowles – to be photographed by Annie Leibowitz for Walt Disney's Year of a Million Dreams campaign. David was Prince Philip, from *Sleeping Beauty*, pictured on a rearing white stallion while brandishing a sword. He was clearly thrilled. 'My sons love the Disney characters and it's a big part of their lives, a big part of many children's lives around the world,' he said. 'I love going to Disney, I'm like a big kid.'

But it wasn't just his commercial activities that were flourishing: so, too, against every piece of advice and accepted wisdom was his career. Football pundits had been quick to dismiss him as a has, been as soon as he signed with the American club, a stance that was hugely reinforced by the announcement that Beckham would never again play for Real Madrid. This had the slightly unexpected benefit of allowing him to rest properly, which meant that when he was, in fact, returned to the field by Real – Capello had been placed under enormous pressure from the fans – he quite suddenly began to show the flair and talent of his early days. Now people started to bemoan the fact that far from his best years being behind him, David Beckham was as good as he'd ever had been – and was going to waste all that talent on an American club. He couldn't win (against his critics, that is), but seemed remarkably unperturbed by the furore raging about him once more.

Indeed, it quickly became known that he would probably have

a chance to once again play for England, too. England manager Steve McClaren admitted as much: 'We have four weeks before the squad is announced [for the Euro 2008 qualifiers] and we will see what happens,' he said. 'He is performing well for his club – obviously that's a problem I would rather have than not have. He has always bounced back from every adversity in his career. It's pleasing to see that a month ago he would never play for Real Madrid again and there he is starring in a game against Bayern Munich and being man of the match.'

David himself was well aware of the debate. 'Football is all about opinions and I know there are some who don't want me in the squad,' he admitted. 'But if people think my England career is over, I want to show it isn't. I'm the underdog now. Eight months ago it was being said that I shouldn't be in the England team any more and my career was over. Even if I look back two or three weeks I wasn't playing for Real Madrid and all of a sudden it's turned around. Of course things would be different if England were winning and almost qualified for Euro 2008, but people always look for other options. I'm not going to lie – I love the fact that I have got the backing of the public – it's a great feeling. We love it in England when we see players determined to prove people wrong. We love it when people fight back – and I've always tried to do that.'

Of course, all this was going down a storm in the Beckhams' home-to-be. David was featured on the cover of the US style magazine *Details*, which called him a hero and, in putting him on the cover, ranked him beside others such as Matt Damon, Brad

Pitt and George Clooney. 'No one is as good at the art of celebrity as David Beckham,' the feature stated. 'Being Americans, we find it hard to accept that one of ours is not at the top of this particular pyramid, but it's true.' If that were not enough, *Details* forecast that he would become an American hero.

In this new mood of bonhomie, it was fitting that this was the moment when David and Sir Alex Ferguson very publicly buried the hatchet. He was invited to Old Trafford to play in a charity game to celebrate United's 50 years in Europe, and although injury stopped him from playing, he was treated as an honoured guest. At half-time he also made a speech: 'It's amazing to be back – I've waited four years for this,' he said. 'I'm devastated I couldn't play, but I wanted to see everyone again and say, "Thank you". Everyone knows you've got the best manager in the world at this club. I've watched the majority of United's games this season on TV in Spain and I'm sure they are going to go on and win many trophies.'

'It's nice of David to say that,' said an equally Sir Alex. 'I expected him to get a great reception from the fans – he was a great player for us.'

It was slightly unfortunate that Sven-Göran Eriksson chose this moment to reveal that he thought Becks was the reason England hadn't won the World Cup: it was not his playing that was to blame but the attitude of his teammates, who were jealous of him. 'Sven told me that the biggest problem he had at the World Cup in Germany last summer was that the other players did not like David Beckham,' said Israeli super agent

Pini Zahavi. 'They did not like the way Beckham was treated like a superstar. That was probably the reason why he was not called up by McClaren when he took over. He told me that the other players did not like Beckham's position in the team as a big, big star. There was a lot of jealousy.'

Even so, Becks was only too keen to come back to the team. At the Sport Industry Awards, where he was honoured for an outstanding contribution to British sport, he said, 'The biggest honour in my career was winning the England captain's armband and giving that up has been very difficult – but I'm always available for my country.' In other words, he still wanted to play for the national team.

Even the then Prime Minister Tony Blair joined in the fuss as he congratulated Becks on his award. 'The phenomenal interest in his move to the United States is a reflection not just of his talent but also of his understanding of the importance of sport as an industry – creating wealth, jobs and driving passion around the world,' he said.

And still the Beckham publicity machine roared on. David treated Victoria to a birthday weekend in Paris; she in turn gave him a birthday night out with various Spice Girls. Both events received massive coverage, along with speculation that the Spice Girls were planning to reform. Also, it was now almost certain that Beckham would be playing for England again as Steve McClaren said that the door was, indeed, open. 'I never said I had closed the door on David,' he protested. 'People will see on Saturday morning what my intentions are.

I keep my eye on all the players. I said from day one I'd continue to monitor David's form – and I have.' Indeed, shortly afterwards, it was announced he was back in the team.

Given the huge amount of publicity that surrounded everything he did, however – not to mention his teammates' jealousy – it was agreed that Becks would give no interviews about his new role. 'David Beckham wants that as well,' said McClaren. 'He just wants to play football. I know David well enough and we want David Beckham the player performing on the field. That's what I've said to him and he agrees with that and that's all we want, him playing. That's why he doesn't want to speak this week. We want to keep it low-key because otherwise there might be that attention. Sometimes it's not the fault of him but people around him, the media and the hype that surrounds David Beckham. We just said, "Let's focus on the next 10 days, and let's make sure he performs."'

Certainly, Beckham was receiving as much media attention as ever. There had been an intense amount of speculation that he was to receive a knighthood, but nervous civil servants were said to have quashed the plans, not least because of the forthcoming move to the States. 'Some officials feel there's nothing wrong with honouring a player based in Europe and free to represent his country if required, but feel there's a big difference if he is earning his main income in the US and unable to play for England,' said a source. There were also concerns that Tony

Blair, now in his last months in office as prime minister, might be seen to be attaching himself to the Beckham bandwagon.

Whatever the cause, the idea was set aside for now.

In the event, David's return to the national team was a resounding success, with him helping England to reach a draw with Brazil. Rather ironically, he was credited not just with inspiring the team to play better, but also with saving Steve McClaren's skin.

In the event, his return to the England team was so successful that Real Madrid publicly voiced regret at letting him go. 'We have all made mistakes regarding Beckham,' said Real president Ramon Calderon. 'Beckham is a great player now he is playing at the same level he did at Manchester. He has recovered his physical and psychological condition because he was upset not to be playing with his national team.'

LA Galaxy, needless to say, was delighted. They 'politely but firmly' rejected attempts by Real to buy him out of his contract: 'Nothing has changed,' said Alexi Lalas, general manager of LA Galaxy. 'We can't wait for Beckham to get here. Real's hopes about keeping Beckham are benign – that ship has sailed.'

Beckham himself was adamant it was time to go. 'My last game will be on Sunday,' he said, just before his last-ever outing with Real Madrid. 'There is no clause in the contract with the LA Galaxy saying things could be changed. Everyone knows my last game is on Sunday. In four years here, the people and the fans have been incredible, but I had to make a decision because after my contract expired on 30 June, it was not going to be renewed and my option was to go to the United States. I could have stayed at Real Madrid for two or three years, for the rest of my career, but things happen. I have lots of respect for the president and Capello, who is one of the best coaches in the world. I respect him, but my Real Madrid career will be over on Sunday.' Ironically, of course, his professional life with Capello was far from over, given the former was to be appointed England coach in the following year. And Capello paid a heavy price for letting David go: a couple of days after Becks' last appearance for the team, he lost his job.

David's last game in Madrid was a triumph: he helped Real to beat Real Mallorca 3–1, as his new friend Tom Cruise watched in the crowd. Meanwhile, Victoria had news of her own – shortly before the family finally made their move to LA, it was announced that the Spice Girls would be reuniting at the end of the year. David, of course, would be there offering his support. The Beckhams' profile, already stratospheric, was about to get bigger still.

CHAPTER 15

AMERICAN IDOL

The arrival of the Beckhams in America resembled not so much a footballer moving from one team to another as a state visit from a reigning monarch – the monarch in this case being the king of celebrity culture and the visit one that would stretch into years. Indeed, there is every chance the Beckhams will make the United States their permanent home: when he has kicked his last football and she has sung her last note, the opportunities there will still be far greater than anywhere else in the world. And by now, the Beckhams had totally transcended what might be called the rational celebrity they deserved: they had become, as Victoria had publicly and famously wished many years earlier, a brand. Not even the sum of their two parts any longer, the couple had achieved uber-fame, and their new countrymen were ecstatic to have them, at long last, there.

They prefaced the move by an interview in *W* magazine,

which made world headlines because of its raunchy shots of the couple: one showed Victoria reclining on the hood of a car as David stood over her. The couple were quizzed on their new £11 million mansion in Beverley Hills – Victoria apparently did the house-hunting, sending pictures of each property to David on her mobile phone. It was a 13,000 square foot six-bedroom villa with a pool, tennis court and cinema room, but it was not, she insisted, too over the top.

'I had quite a lot of things to get my head around,' she said. 'What was the nicest area? I was very much like, "Okay, the seaside is down there, training is there, school is there, and I think Barneys is over there". I kind of did it like that. We didn't want anything too huge, too fancy, too ostentatious.' The goal, she said, was 'something quite practical for the kids. It's a light, happy house, with a great corridor the kids are going to love when they are roller-skating.'

She was also adamant that the move had nothing to do with their profile abroad. 'We're not out to be the most famous people in America,' she said. 'We're not looking at the move as boosting the brand. We're us and we've got our kids. We're not aware of a lot of the madness going on around us. We kind of keep to ourselves, really.'

She also talked forthrightly about the Rebecca Loos affair. 'I'm not going to lie. It was a really tough time,' she said. 'It was hard for our entire families. But I realised a lot of people have a price. David and I got through it together. No one said marriage was going to be easy. Yes, there have been bumps along the road. But the fact is we've come out of everything we've been through stronger and happier. It's even better now than when we were first married. After all these years, we can just come home and have a laugh together.'

David was also happy to talk about his constantly changing image, and won massive brownie points for (again) saying how pleased he was to be a gay icon. 'I never actually think, okay, next week I'm going to get a mullet,' he said. 'I just wake up one morning and I'm bored with my hair and shave it off. It's just something I enjoy. I've always had a liking towards clothes, but when I met Victoria, she directed me in the right way. When she tells me something doesn't look good, I believe her. We have a connection that way.' As for the gay fan base – 'I feel it's an honour,' he said. 'It's nice to be loved.'

The world's press converged on LA Galaxy as Beckham held a press conference to announce his arrival. A newly-blonde Victoria was present, looking resplendent in a pink Roland Mouret moon dress, a full five months before it was available in the shops. 'Thank you for making my dream come true,' David began. 'My family have now moved to Los Angeles and it is something we look forward to and are proud of. In our life, everything is perfect. The most important thing in my life is my family, but the second is football, sorry, soccer – I have to get used to that. In my career I have played for two of the biggest clubs in the world in Manchester United and Real Madrid. I have played for my country for the last 11 years and I still am. I have always looked for challenges and something exciting and this is one of the biggest challenges I have ever taken in my career. Soccer in America could potentially be as big as anywhere in the world. I am proud to be part of trying to help the sport grow for the next five years and possibly longer.' Possibly longer. It was a clear sign that the family was sure where their future lay.

Sensibly, Beckham tried to play it all down. 'The hype is there at the moment and the hype will be there for maybe six months,' he said in an interview with *Sports Illustrated*. 'But to keep the interest in soccer – that's going to be the challenge. I'm not silly enough to think I'm going to change the whole culture, because it's not going to happen. But I do have a belief that soccer can go to a different level and I'd love to be a part of that. People do think they're going to see me turn out and we'll win our first game 10-0. That's one thing I'm worried about. I'm not a player who will run past 10 players and score three or four goals. My game is about working hard, being a team player and assists.'

It must be said, not everyone was enthusiastic about the move. Quite a few jokes were made at the couple's expense on late-night talk shows, while Victoria's documentary about the move, *Coming To America*, was panned on both sides of the Atlantic. Worse still, David's new team put in a dreadful performance shortly after his arrival, losing 3-0 to the Mexican team Tigres. Beckham himself was unable to play thanks to a strained ankle, but observers noticed he watched the game with a slightly surprised air, perhaps fully understanding for the first time quite the change he had made in his life as a player. David had, after all, spent his entire professional life playing for two of the best teams in the world, not a category LA Galaxy could fit into. Nor did the team bosses pretend it was a triumphant start. 'That was a miserable performance and not something we will ever be proud of,' said Alexi Lalas, the club president. 'David knows there is some quality out there and with the addition of him, the team can go on and be successful.'

It was an awfully big burden for one person to bear – indeed, David was being spoken of as not just the saviour of LA Galaxy, but the man who would transform the status of American soccer worldwide – but he, himself, seemed unperturbed. One of the reasons he and Victoria have been able to cope with life in the limelight for so long – and they have coped, despite the occasional hiccup – is that both retained a grounded quality, and this stood him in very good stead now. He was there on behalf of US Major League Soccer, he maintained. 'It's about me being the ambassador of MLS,' he said. 'People are talking about me going into the movies and Hollywood. It's not what I am here for. I am here to play football.'

Hollywood itself, however, was overjoyed to welcome the new arrivals as its own. The Beckhams' new great friends Tom Cruise and Katie Holmes hosted a party in their honour at the Museum of Contemporary Art's Geffen Contemporary Gallery, which was so A-list it made the Oscars look devoid of stars. Attendees included Will Smith and his wife Jada Pinkett Smith, Demi Moore, Bruce Willis, Jim Carrey, Eva Longoria, Brooke Shields and the film director Ron Howard. Helicopters flew overhead and a red carpet was rolled out for the guests, while onlookers were held back by the police. Inside, the gallery, normally somewhat cavernous, had been transformed into a nightclub: sofas, flowers and extravagant lighting glittered everywhere. The doubters would say what they liked about David's new team, but when it came to what Hollywood really recognized – celebrity and wealth – the Beckhams had arrived at their spiritual home.

The football was almost irrelevant by this stage, but one man who had seen it all and done it all before issued a warning note. The Brazilian footballer Pelé, widely regarded as the greatest player ever, had trod the same path as David when he joined the New York Cosmos 30-odd years previously, and counseled David to remember why he was there. Practise must come before partying, he said. 'David Beckham is more of a pop star than a player,' he said. 'From my experience with New York Cosmos, I would advise him to be very well prepared for the matches. I know the level of play in the league. It is well balanced, and the spectators will demand a lot from him as their star player. But when there's no training or practice, then he can stroll through Hollywood.'

Sir Alex Ferguson felt exactly the same way. 'They have already had Pelé, Cruyff and Beckenbauer out there,' he said. 'I don't know what kind of impact David can make. He can't change the whole country, and the sheer size of the place makes it more difficult.'

And indeed, while the Beckhams were now bona fide A-listers, the reason for their being in LA, the soccer, was still not going so well. There was mounting dissatisfaction from the fans that David's sprained ankle had kept him off the field and so, although it was not yet healed, he finally made an appearance in the 78th minute of a game, touching the ball only 12 times. The man said to be behind his appearance was Simon Fuller, he who had first introduced the Spice Girls to the world, and he who now managed Brand Beckham.

'Brand Beckham needed their star on the field and Simon made sure it happened,' said a source. 'For the thousands of extra seats sold that day, the hundreds of thousands of seats sold at stadiums across America anticipating Beckham's arrival, for all the licensed merchandise, endorsements and to keep the hype alive, he needed to be on the field. And Simon is producing a new TV series following Beckham's progress in American soccer, which began airing this week. It would be a disappointing premiere if Beckham spent his first game on the sidelines icing his ankle. That's not exciting TV.'

Beckham ignored it all and worked on improving his fitness, but everything was brought down to earth with a very sharp bump when his father Ted, then 59, suffered a heart attack. The two had not been as close as they once were in years, but this put everything in very sharp perspective. The entire clan moved to be at Ted's side, at

Whipps Cross Hospital in east London, Beckham included, who boarded the first plane he could. 'David is frantic with worry,' said a friend. 'His family are all rushing from wherever they are to be with Ted. David is on the first available flight and will be in London as soon as he can. He's travelling through the night. There's no secret the pair haven't always seen eye-to-eye – but that's all in the past. When something like this happens, any son would drop everything to be with his father.'

He was first off the BA flight when it arrived in London, and was escorted from the plane by two waiting officials, from where, clearly upset, he was driven straight to the hospital, arriving at 1.30pm.

'David walked in through a side entrance and went straight to his dad's bedside,' said an observer. 'He was not crying, but he did look close to tears. He looked really pensive and desperate to see his dad.'

Victoria had been working in Japan, promoting her cosmetics range, but to her credit she, too, dropped all her plans and headed straight back to London. The usual circus promptly descended on the hospital: a fight broke out when hospital staff tried to stop someone from entering because they thought he was a photographer, when he was, in fact, part of the Beckham entourage.

Ted himself, however, soon began to make a recovery. 'He is conscious and talking, and that's a positive step,' said the Beckhams' spokesman, Simon Oliviera. 'It's too early to say how long David and Victoria will be here. They will stay as long as it takes and as long as Ted needs them.'

In the event, Ted made a rapid recovery. Four days after they arrived in London, the Beckhams were able to return to LA, leaving a much improved Ted saying 'I'll be OK' and waving the couple off from the car park. 'David was very sweet and brought Ted some home-made fruit punch and a salad,' said a source at the hospital. 'Posh even took off her sunglasses when she reached the ward.'

Although Ted made a full recovery, it was a salutary warning about what was really important in the couple's lives. David and Ted had already been partially reconciled after the rows following his divorce from Sandra and the publication of his book, but father and son were now close once more. Ted acknowledged as much. 'All three of my children David, Lynne and Joanne have been a tower of strength,' he said. 'They have helped me get through this along with the doctors and nurses. I owe a lot to all of them.'

The speed with which Victoria flew to be at her husband's side was also the harbinger of a new period of closeness between the pair. Victoria had her own concerns bubbling in the background: she was preparing for the Spice Girls' reunion tour, amid fears that she might be too physically weak to carry off the demanding stage routines. Her slimness, after all, was due to her diet, not her exercise regime. David decided to take her in hand. 'He has told her he can build up her fitness over the next few weeks at home, where no one can see or photograph them,' said a friend. 'It will make a big difference. But the key is she has to listen to him. David feels he can help to calm her down and assuage her anxieties. His main objective is to build up her stamina and her core muscle strength. He will get her on the mat doing press-ups to strengthen her arms and horizontal cycling to build up her leg strength. He's also putting her on the bike for 10-minute bursts of fast pedalling plus sit-ups to strengthen her abs.'

Indeed, for the first time in many years, the focus appeared increasingly to be on Victoria's career, not David's. The Spice Girls reunion was attracting a huge amount of publicity, while David's first season with LA Galaxy had proven to be something of a damp squib. David was feeling it, too. 'David is depressed because he is not playing football, and that is the nature of the man,' said Tim Lovejoy, who had made several television programmes about him. 'Everybody always goes on about the commercial ventures and says that what he is about, but he is not. He just wants to play football. That's what it is about.'

Not that everything was running smoothly on that front back in Britain, either. The new England coach Steve McClaren – who was shortly to lose his job – was incurring the wrath of just about everyone as the team openly floundered, and nor was he making use of the talent at his disposal. David was first very publicly dropped from a vital Euro 2008 qualifier against Croatia in November 2007, but was then brought on as a second-half substitute after all. He very nearly managed to save the team from defeat, but it was not to be: England were beaten 3-2, signalling the end of the team's Euro 2008 ambitions and, indeed, Steve McClaren's job as England manager.

The person who displayed the greatest maturity about all this was Beckham himself. He had, after all, experienced enough of the highs and lows of the game himself over the years, and spoke out in defence of the younger and less experienced players, who were being blamed for the defeat. 'Without a doubt, we are disappointed and we are hurting – every one of those players,' he said. 'They might be young, but they've all played in big games, they all play for big teams. I've captained many of those players and I know how much it hurts them, and I know how much it hurts them to just lose a tackle, let alone lose a game and be knocked out.'

But David's own star remained undiminished. As the year drew to a close, he was one of a very select few to appear on Michael Parkinson's last ever chat show, along with the likes of Billy Connolly and Dame Judi Dench, confirming his growing status as national treasure. He had also, courtesy of the Croatia match, won his 99th cap for England, and now seemed almost assured of a coveted 100th when he was named as the official face of the FA's bid to host the World Cup in 2018. Given that he had also been involved in England's successful bid to host the 2012 Olympics, he was clearly now a well-regarded figure within the sporting establishment, as well as one of its greatest players.

On the *Parkinson* show, he talked again about the obsessive-compulsive behaviour that had plagued him for so many years. 'In our house in Spain we used to have this big rug that when you hoovered it, you could do it in lines like Wembley,' he said. 'Victoria used to catch me after the kids had gone to bed, doing the hoovering, and it would all be in perfect lines. I have to have everything in the right place and she finds it very annoying. Also cans of drinks in the fridge...I have to have four, four, four instead of four, five, four. Odd things like that she has remarked upon.'

He also talked emotionally about stepping down as England captain. 'I remember waking up that morning and I cried as I knew what I was going to have to do,' he said. 'I went into the press conference, cried all the way down to it, got through it and cried all the way back to the hotel. But I have had a great career on the England side. [But] I won't be retiring yet. I believe I have two or three years yet, but I will never be a manager.'

He wasn't above putting on a rather bold front, however. In December 2007, he signed a three-year, £20 million contract to become Armani 'ambassador', the first contract of its kind for any sportsman. 'He represents a notion of modern masculinity, as a sports hero, husband and father,' said Giorgio Armani. 'Soccer players were not always considered to be fashion role models. David Beckham has helped to change that.'

In the event, his first appearance for the brand was an eye-popping one. David appeared, in all his glory, with what was termed the 'Goldenballs lunchbox' right out there in a bulging pair of skimpy briefs. The picture didn't leave a lot to the imagination and it divided the nation sharply between those who thought David had never appeared to better effect and those who thought it vulgar beyond belief.

Whatever the vulgar brigade thought, it worked. Sales of Armani underwear rose by a staggering 30 per cent in the wake of the picture, while sales of men's underwear generally soared. It was the Beckham effect in action once again. 'David Beckham is a global style icon, appealing equally to men and women,' said David Walker-Smith, Selfridges' head of menswear. 'Where he goes, fashion is bound to follow, so briefs are the big story for underwear.'

Victoria, by now in the middle of the extremely successful Spice Girls reunion tour, had her own take on events. 'I sleep naked,' she said. 'I'm going to be naked if I'm getting in bed with David every night. There are so many – and I hate the word – "celebrities"' clothing lines and fragrances but most of them have nothing to do with it. I'm so camp. I'm such a gay man trying to get out. I don't give a fuck what anybody thinks!'

She had also, for the first time in years, appeared to have put on a little weight. 'Victoria wanted to bulk up a little for the tour – and it has paid off,' said a friend. 'It's the first time in years that she has tried to gain weight. Initially, it was only so she could cope with the strain of the tour, but she's feeling full of energy and likes her curvier look. David's very excited about

Posh's weight gain. He has told her how pleased he is…and how sexy she looks.'

At this juncture it was announced that none other than Fabio Capello was to take over as England manager. Amongst the numerous other topics this presented to the pundits was what his appointment would mean for Beckham, not least because as manager of Real Madrid, he had briefly sidelined David. The answer appeared to be that he would be happy to have David back in the team. 'He accepted he had made a mistake and was big enough to admit it,' said Ruud Gullit, the Dutch footballer who had played under Capello at AC Milan in the early 1990s. 'So I have no doubt he would not stand in the way of letting Beckham get 100 caps.'

The choice went down well with Victoria. 'I think it's great that Capello is the new England manager,' she said. 'David has a lot of respect for him.'

As the year drew to a close, there were rumours that Victoria was pregnant once more. The couple were widely known to want to add a daughter to their brood, but Victoria herself was keen to put paid to those rumours. 'I'm not pregnant,' she told CNN's Larry King. 'At the moment, the children I've got keep me very, very busy. They actually put me in goal and kick footballs with me – I'm the goalie of the family. At some point a little girl would be great but right now I just want to enjoy the children that I've got.'

Asked why she didn't smile a bit more – and given that recent picture of her husband, pundits were quipping she had a fair amount to smile about – she replied, 'I don't know why because I really like to have a laugh.

'I have quite a dry sense of humour. I think that's just the way that I look in pictures. I know I look very miserable and I have to try and smile more, which is ironic really, because I'm quite a funny sort of person. So, you know, I will try.'

She was certainly enjoying herself at the time. The Spice Girls were now playing the O2 Arena, with tickets said to be changing hands on the black market at up to £1,000 a time. Each member had a solo moment in the show: Victoria alone didn't sing in hers, but was shown strutting across the stage: she got the biggest cheers of the night. David, meanwhile, had been in attendance throughout much of the tour, being termed, inevitably, a 'Spice Boy'.

The Italian designer Roberto Cavalli, who had put together the spectacular costumes for the tour, was also on the receiving end of much praise. 'I asked them about their bodies, what they wanted to show and hide, and about how they had evolved since they were Spice Girls,' he said. '[Victoria] was the most daring. She wanted to experiment, to surprise and be different. Her only request was that we give her hips.'

The person behind the tour was none other than Simon Fuller. The girls famously sacked him as their manager first time around and lived to regret it; these days, however, all was harmony. Fuller was now in charge of David as well as Victoria and the girls were all keen to emphasise all was sweetness and light.

'It's very respectful,' said Mel B. 'He listens more this time.'

'It's good,' added Victoria. 'We all realised that to make this work it's not just about us. A lot of people make this work and Simon has done a really good job. He's the best at what he does.'

'I read somewhere that he wasn't allowing us complimentary tickets for our friends and family – so not true,' said Emma.

'We have complete control,' said Mel B.

The Beckham effect was making itself known in other ways, too. LA Galaxy might not have been having much luck on the pitch, but their merchandising was certainly doing well off it: 300,000 Beckham jerseys had been sold, with sales of shirts 700 times more than usual. 'Merchandise sales overall have gone up two or three times,' said Don Gerber, the head of Major League Soccer. 'International TV sales have gone up from next to nothing to distribution in 100 countries, with live games in Asia and Mexico. Major League Soccer has more global awareness than at any other time in our history because of David. But the real value we've yet to realise is the impact David will have on the field. He's been injured, but we look forward to him having another first year in MLS in 2008.'

Christmas 2007 was spent back in the UK. The Spice Girls were performing in London and Beckingham Palace was convenient for all the parents, so it was natural the family should be in situ for the time of year. They all seemed to be enjoying it: a proud David was spotted skating with Romeo at the Winter Wonderland rink in London's Hyde Park – Victoria stayed at the side.

CHAPTER 16

BACK TO BASICS

In the wake of his move to LA Galaxy, many commentators had been of the opinion that David's glory days as a sportsman were over. Not for the first time, he proved them wrong. In January 2008, in the American close season, David asked for and got Arsenal manager Arsène Wenger's permission to train with Arsenal, with the direct aim of impressing Fabio Capello, the new England coach.

'He is working to be fit before moving back to Los Angeles in February, so now, in January, we are giving him assistance with his fitness,' said Wenger. It was a sign that although Beckham relished the life of an international megastar (and Los Angeles was the right place to be for that role), he was still taking his football deadly seriously. The game was most certainly not up for Beckham yet.

Indeed, he was at pains to express his admiration for Capello. 'Apart from Sir Alex Ferguson, I have never seen anyone so dedicated to watching football and learning about it,' he said. 'He will do it his way and that is a good thing. We had the fear factor the year we won La Liga. That is what all great managers have. The fear factor with a manager is important. We had it at Manchester United with Sir Alex Ferguson, and he had so much success and is still having it. Fabio Capello has an aura that players will enjoy. I enjoyed playing under him, even in the bad times.' But he was determined there wouldn't be too many of those.

The clout that Beckham now wielded absolutely everywhere he went was apparent on that trip to the UK. He was pictured visiting the new prime minister, Gordon Brown, at 10 Downing Street, and the following day the PM returned the favour and visited David's football academy. He also attended a dinner in his honour held by the Football Writers' Association, an occasion he used to heap praise upon his family and friends. That was followed by a trip to Sierra Leone in his capacity as a goodwill ambassador for Unicef, which he used to highlight the plight of suffering children. Clearly, he wanted to give something back to a world that had given him so much. 'I'm a footballer,' he told one journalist. 'A lot of people are aware of what I'm doing and they listen to what I say. I want to make awareness of what Unicef is doing bigger. And I've always thought there was something more for me to do with my life than just play football.' He certainly did his bit: along with visiting a health clinic, he engaged in a game of football with the local boys.

Beckham admitted that it did bring it home quite how privileged his own life was, but said that he and Victoria did everything they could to keep it as normal as possible. They might have bodyguards everywhere, but the children were not spoilt. 'Our boys are very grounded,' he said. 'Me and Victoria feel we've been brought up in the right way so that's how we should bring up our boys. We're very strict with discipline; they all take their plates to the dishwasher. They don't get anything without saying please and thank you, and our proudest moments are when people comment on their good manners. Some people with our sort of lives let their nannies do everything. Of course we have nannies but whatever we're doing we make sure one of us is at home. We want our children to know we're their mummy and daddy – and they do. They're quite like I was as a kid – sensitive but knowing what they want and trying to get it.'

David also gave a rather telling insight into other aspects of his life, talking about his mother. 'If we're round at hers for Sunday dinner, she can't relax until the washing-up's done – then she'll sit down,' he said. 'I'm the same. I am a very, very tidy person. That's really true! But I believe that no one can clean the house and make the beds like me – that's all part of obsessive-compulsive disorder. I have to have my clothes ready for the next morning. It's not that I want to look my best because I'm pictured every time I go out. It's what I've always done.'

Old wounds were beginning to heal. There had been an

immense amount of speculation as to whether Fabio Capello would allow David to play for England and thus win his 100th cap: none other than Sir Alex Ferguson backed David for the honour. It had been five years since their relationship had fallen apart, and both were now keen to hark back to the glory days they had spent together. Anyway, in Sir Alex's eyes, David had redeemed himself: while his new team might not be in the league he had formerly played in, Becks himself was clearly determined to keep himself on a world class level.

Even so, it didn't quite work. Just as David was launching his David Beckham World Of Sport resort near Natal in Brazil, the news emerged that Capello hadn't picked him after all. David was clearly disappointed, but asserted that he wasn't going to give up on his international career just yet: he intended to keep on fighting for a role in the team.

'If I'm not in [the squad], that's life,' he said. 'Who knows whether I'll call it a day. But I don't think I will because I have always said I want to be available. That's what I did when Steve McClaren dropped me [in August 2006]. Deep down, I did not think I would ever play for England again. So to be on 99 caps is great. It's more than I dreamt of. If I am not in the squad, I will carry on working hard and trying to get back in. I won't get bitter and twisted because I am old enough and I have got enough respect for the manager to realise that if it does not happen, life goes on. When you get that first cap, you don't want it to end there. Sometimes, it does. That's the worry inside. It's like when I was captain for the first time. I didn't want to be captain for one game. I wanted to carry on.' He did and in March 2008 bagged his 100th England cap – wearing a pair of gold boots to mark the occasion. Ted Beckham was there to watch – his earlier illness had clearly brought the family together again.

Days afterwards he was back in the States, playing with LA Galaxy (they lost 4-0 to the Colorado Rapids), but he continued to charm the US. He appeared on Jay Leno's chat show, where he was quizzed about the Armani ad in which he appeared in very brief briefs and nothing else: 'Is that how you relax at home?' asked Leno.

'No, definitely not,' said a slightly flustered David. 'I was so nervous about doing that campaign because obviously I've done photoshoots before but never actually in my underwear. To do that I was quite nervous because obviously I knew my wife and friends were going to see it – but my mum was going to see it! When the photos first came out she was the first one to call and say "What are you doing?" I had to try to explain it to her but it didn't really go down that well.'

America loved it and they perked up even more when LA Galaxy won 2-0 over San Jose. It wasn't just those in the States following David's career, either: he had made it clear he wanted to go on playing for England, and so every triumph or tragedy on the pitch gave rise to more intense speculation in the British press about how long he would be able to go on. His earning potential was as high as ever: in April 2008, he was named as football's best-paid player, with an impressive

£24.7 million a year since joining LA Galaxy. If nothing else, the move was making him an even richer man.

It was also doing wonders for the profile of American football. 'What he has done is bring so much more attention to the game as a whole,' said Bob Bradley, coach of the United States team. 'There are so many non-soccer fans in the USA that are now more aware of our game because of his presence. For many years good things have gone on when it comes to soccer – we have made our mark in World Cup final stages – but it doesn't always get the attention in the US, where the coverage is so competitive. We've got great teams in many sports. But when the spotlight of Beckham goes on I think people take more notice of the things that have been happening in our game. I expect we will see him at Wembley. Fabio Capello still feels he can play and help the team. His run of form so far in MLS has been good and his pure ability to deliver passes and open up the field is something that all managers would love to have.'

He was right: David did appear at Wembley, playing against his adopted country. Fabio Capello followed that up by installing him as team captain for a friendly against Trinidad and Tobago and publicly voicing his support: 'If he remains physically fit, then it's possible he will still be a big player for us in the World Cup,' he said. 'He is also one of the five or six candidates in the frame to do the captaincy job permanently. I know David Beckham very well. I had one year with him at Real Madrid. He is a leader of other players.' David had been making it clear that he wanted to continue his international career: it looked as if he was going to get his wish. This was his 59th outing as captain and his 102nd England cap.

David's status as one of the foremost stars on the planet was confirmed in June 2008, when he was placed at number five in the Forbes annual celebrity list in order of power (Victoria, with the Spice Girls, was at number 50). Even so, he was increasingly aware that his career at the top of football couldn't last forever. 'I won't get a phone call when I'm left out, and I won't expect one,' he said. 'There are managers who do that. Sir Alex Ferguson would pull you in on a Saturday morning and give you a reason for dropping you, even if you'd be telling him that you wanted to play, that you weren't tired. But with the manager [Capello] I could be sitting at home one day and not be in the squad and it is all over, and I won't complain.

'I just need to know that I have done as much as I can. I wouldn't like to say I have enjoyed my recent caps more than previous ones because I've been very proud of them all. But the fact that people doubted my age, then the fact that I was playing in the USA and I'm still out there playing for my country, and captaining them, well it is good to know I can still prove people wrong. I've always enjoyed doing that. I didn't think I would be here. When I was left out [by Steve McClaren] at the start of the Euro [2008] qualifiers, I just thought "that's it, that's my England career done". So it is not a question of taking it or leaving it now. It is just that I have seen before how quickly it can all get taken away from you.'

But it hadn't gone yet. Becks' stock was high with the fans: in May 2008, LA Galaxy beat Kansas City Wizards 3-1, giving them their first winning record in two years and moving the club into first place in the Western Conference. In the course of the match, Becks scored an empty net goal from 70 yards out, the second time in his career that he had scored from inside his own half.

The full measure of Beckham's international appeal again became apparent in August 2008, when he performed on the top of a double-decker bus for eight minutes as part of the Beijing Olympics closing session in the Bird's Nest stadium. This was in part because the 2012 Olympics were to be held in London, David's home city, and he had played a role in securing the games; he took part in the closing ceremony in Beijing and he would also be taking part in the opening ceremony in London. On top of that, he was not only Britain's most famous footballer, but the world's most famous footballer. He was the obvious choice.

David continued to play football at the highest level, too. In moving to LA Galaxy, he had provoked comment to the effect that he was choosing celebrity over skill and, indeed, no one would have said that he was transferring to the world's best team. However, somehow he managed to confound the critics, and so it was announced in October 2008 that he would be loaned out to AC Milan the following January. Milan had been interested in him at the time he moved to LA Galaxy: now they had finally got their man.

By this time Becks had managed to accumulate 108 England caps and the loan spell in Italy was clearly a way of ensuring he would notch up yet more. Fabio Capello was certainly pleased about the move. 'Milan have made a good addition,' he said. 'At Madrid I left him out of the squad because he had signed a contract with Los Angeles but he continued to come on the field and train and I put him back in the team. He is a very serious lad, very sensible, a professional. People think he is a playboy off the field, it's not true at all.'

Galaxy's coach Bruce Arena approved of the move too, despite the fact that if David suffered an injury, it could have an impact on the way he played with LA Galaxy. 'I think when players don't go 100 per cent they get hurt, so I'm not going to give him any advice about pulling out of tackles,' he said. 'David's a very experienced player and he understands when to go into challenges and when not to.

'Once in a while it doesn't always work out that way but if he goes and can play and train in that environment against players of that quality, it can't be at 50 per cent. He needs to play at 100 per cent and he needs to position himself to get on the field for first-team minutes. Players can get injured whether they are in training camp or playing games and there's no method you can create that can prevent injury.'

The move was not welcomed by everyone, however, with some accusations that taking Beckham on was more a marketing move than anything else. But as soon as David got there, he took his training so seriously that he was soon sent out to play, scoring in his third game, 4-1 against Bologna. From that moment on he had Italy eating out of the palm of his hand.

'I think a lot of people were sceptical at the start because Milan almost admitted at first it was a publicity thing more than football,' said Italian historian John Foot, who wrote *Calcio: A History of Italian Football*. 'A lot of journalists have been surprised that Beckham is actually quite good at football and not many are still waiting to be won over. I saw a piece by a senior Italian journalist recently who said that they kind of expected a male model and instead got a worker.'

The fans were won round, too. 'I don't like the part of him not involved with soccer, I've always thought that it was too much, showbiz overcoming the games,' said one on the AC Milan website. 'People in the stadium don't care about his celebrity as long as it doesn't affect the way he plays. And it hasn't, because he has given a great contribution and become one of our most important players.'

The captain of the team, Paolo Maldini, was pleased. 'Beckham is a great champion, but we shouldn't forget that he has come into a great team and a great club like Milan,' he said when he joined, as David hadn't played for more than two months at that stage. 'We players don't care what his life is like off the pitch, we have found a lad who has not trained for two and a half months, but I have had the chance to talk to him and I noticed his determination and his great desire to put himself to work immediately to return to playing as soon as possible.'

David himself was delighted. 'Going to Milan has been one of the best things that has ever happened to me,' he said.

Even the club doctor, Jean Pierre Meersseman loved him. 'He will be at his top level in 15 to 20 days,' he enthused. 'The tests which he did showed he is already very good. He has an exceptional physique which will allow him, as happened to Maldini or Costacurta, to play for another five or six years.' By that time David would be nearing 40, far older than most footballers managed to hang on.

Back in the States, however, everyone was not so thrilled. It had been a magnificent coup to get him in the first place, but now there was the feeling that perhaps he still realized he could play for better teams. 'It's like a bad break-up, with Beckham having dumped the Galaxy as soon as a prettier girl – in this case AC Milan – showed some interest,' said the football journalist Richard Manfredi, who was based in LA. 'There's a lot of resentment towards Beckham right now, with people feeling that he paid lip service to 'building the sport in America', when his actions show that he was never really committed. If anything, his success at AC Milan has just made it all worse, because now people are wondering if he was just coasting while he was here.'

In fact, he wasn't. David was helping to keep LA Galaxy in the news in a way that club had never been before, and not just because of his own high profile. The standard of play was noticeably higher than it had been previously. It was just that David now had to manage one of the trickier balancing acts of his life.

CHAPTER 17

TO MILAN AND BEYOND

And so the pattern was set that was to dictate David's life from then on: dividing his time between Milan, where football dominated, and LA, where his celebrity continued to grow. Despite everything his critics said about the fame drowning the football, however, Becks continued to astound, and in March 2009 he surpassed Bobby Moore's total of 108 England caps to notch up the most appearances for England of any outfield player.

There were, however, some disappointments. The David Beckham Academy football school, which had opened with great fanfare in 2005 in London and Los Angeles, and which had been planning to expand to Brazil and Asia, was not proving the success that everyone hoped. At the end of 2009, it was announced that the two sites would close, although the London branch would still be a training venue in the run-up to the 2012 Olympics as had been previously planned. Instead, the academy would become a mobile operation. 'The academy is moving beyond one site to a coaching model that can reach more children in communities across the UK and internationally,' said a spokesman for AEG Europe, which owned the site, in a statement in late 2009. 'David Beckham and senior coaching staff are currently developing these ambitious programmes and further news on that front will follow.'

David continued to take some stick from Galaxy fans, being met with signs saying 'Go home fraud' and 'Part-time player' when he returned from Milan. He had, after all, missed the first half of the season, but given that LA Galaxy's performance improved very swiftly after his return, everyone soon calmed down. LA Galaxy rose from third to first in the Western Conference, which eased matters slightly when it was announced that David would allowed to go on loan again to AC Milan in 2010. This duly happened, with the result that in February 2010, David ended up playing against Manchester United for the first time since he left the club in 2003. United won, 3-2. However, his next game with Milan, against Chievo Verona, resulted in him being out of action for months to come, and in him also missing that summer's World Cup. David tore his left Achilles tendon and was subsequently operated on by Doctor Sakari Orava, one of the top surgeons for sportsmen in the world, in Turku, Finland. The operation was deemed a success, but it was not until September that David was able to return to the field.

He did, however, accompany the England squad to South Africa, where he acted as an ambassador and mentor to the younger players.

But his stock as a footballer was as high as ever. As well as playing with Milan, West Ham United were after him: chairman David Gold made it plain that there was an open invitation for David to come on loan to the club or to join them as club ambassador. But with the slightly shocking announcement in late summer that Beckingham Palace was to go on the market, it seemed clearer than ever that the Beckhams now regarded LA as their permanent base.

Becks's international career now hangs in the balance – but then it has done before. It was possibly as well for the man himself that he was unable to play in the 2010 World Cup, given the lacklustre performance put in by his teammates, but in the aftermath of that, Fabio Capello yet again made it clear that David's continuing presence on the team was by no means a given. This had acted as a spur to David to prove himself in the past, and it did so again now.

'I'm not ready to step aside,' he said. 'If I don't get picked for England again then I'm very proud of my record, 100 starts and 115 games. I'm very proud of that but I still believe I have a part to play. I take each day, week, month and year as it comes. Like I say, I never want to step down from playing for my country.'

Steven Gerrard certainly didn't think it was the end, saying that David had 'legendary status' among the supporters. 'I'm sure that if he hears that news, it will drive him on and he'll try to prove people wrong and try to get back in the set-up because I know he loves playing for England,' he said. 'He's put a long shift in as an England player. He's had some fantastic performances, some fantastic goals, memories. I've learnt a lot from David and it's been a pleasure to play alongside him.'

David's personal image continued to be as different from a traditional footballer as could be. When in Milan, he used his spare time to increase his skills in the kitchen, hardly the usual course of action for a man at the very height of his fame in the macho world of sport. But it hadn't stopped him from doing what he wanted in the past and it didn't stop him now.

'I have joined a culinary school and I'm on a course that entails 120 hours of lessons and cooking,' he said. 'It's something that I have always wanted to do. I have always loved cooking. Now I'm Italy, I want to learn how to make amazing pasta. It's gone from a small ambition of wanting to learn how to make pasta to the extreme of doing this course that professional chefs do. It's something I'm passionate about. I did the first three hours the other day. I learned how to make fresh pasta, ragu, carbonara, fresh tomato sauce and I am doing a risotto in a few days.

'I don't know about cooking for a group of people at a dinner party quite yet but you never know. I'm really pleased about it. I'd love to cook for Gordon [Ramsay]. One day, I will definitely cook for him.'

His domestic life continued to be settled, too. 'We always planned to get the kids a dog, but Victoria said "let's wait until you finish at Milan",' he told one interviewer in early 2010. 'But then I was doing some shopping on my own before Christmas [in the UK] and I saw Coco in the shop. I have always wanted a bulldog so as soon as Victoria and the kids arrived back in England, I took them to Harrods and they fell in love with her, too. We asked Gordon to look after her for a short time because she had a virus and she wasn't well enough to travel back to LA with the family. It cost £1,500 to get her to the US and now she's one of the family.'

Beckham's status as an icon is not in doubt, so much so that in March 2010 he flew out from the Royal Air Force base at Brize Norton in Oxfordshire to visit British troops in Afghanistan. 'I have nothing but admiration for these young men and women and it makes me very proud to be British,' Beckham said. A Ministry of Defence spokeswoman seemed equally pleased: 'This is a long-planned morale-boosting trip for the benefit of our troops during which he will meet service personnel from all the services as well as international and Afghan troops,' she said.

David certainly did his bit. He was taken to Camp Bastion, Helmand Province, where temperatures were about 45°C, where he posed for pictures and signed autographs with the troops, as well as being given lessons in how to handle the weapons. David had always displayed a fierce patriotism throughout his career and that was certainly on display now.

He might have been the iconic one present at the camp, but he left onlookers in no doubt as to who he thought really deserved respect.

'You know I've been here just one night so far and the experience has been even more than I could have ever hoped,' he told BFBS: British Forces News. 'To see the morale of the troops is really incredible. It first kind of hit me on the way over when we were on the military plane flying in to Afghanistan. You can see the faces, you can see obviously they know they are leaving their families, but they're so focused and they've got this look in their eyes that they're just so confident and just ready. That really is an unbelievable sight to see, and you feel it as well. Just yesterday one of the troops was killed, and you feel it and you see the flags at half-mast and you feel the tension there. It really is, like I said, amazing to be around but you feel the love from everybody. It just really is scary work. These guys are the bravest people that I've ever met and it really is, it truly is, an honour to be here.'

David was following in a long and honourable tradition of entertainers cheering up the men in the field, but he was taking some personal risk. Foreign Secretary William Hague and Defence Secretary Liam Fox were both out there as well, and with such high profile men in the area, there was a real danger that they would be targeted by the Taliban. Indeed, there was a surprise Taliban attack on Kandahar airfield when they were all there. 'The Taliban could not resist the chance of taking out one of these VIPs,' said a source. 'They weren't to know none of the three men were at Kandahar. It was one of the obvious places to have a go.'

Beckham got home safely, though, and was soon told by Fabio Capello that the door was always open for him to come and play for England again. That put an end to West Ham's hopes of securing Beckham's services: 'It was a possibility and we really did try to get him, but we have not heard back,' said club owner David Gold. 'It would appear he has gone on to other things and now we have to move on too.'

Meanwhile, Capello was sounding positively conciliatory. 'I have spoken with David on the telephone and explained what happened – and the relationship between him and me is really good,' he said by way of explanation. 'First he has to be back playing. We have to look at the young players for the future but we will be monitoring all the players. The door is open for all players. No one player is out.'

Over in the States, the Beckham offspring were becoming baseball aficionados, and were pictured playing with their father, his mate Gordon Ramsay and Gordon's son Jack. They were also following basketball. Victoria's career, meanwhile, was also going from strength to strength: now firmly established as a fashion designer, she as much as anyone wanted the family to continue with their new life in the United States.

David was also as happy to portray himself as a very unusual footballer indeed in the States, as in the UK. 'I've always liked to look elegant,' he told a US sports channel. 'I've always been into looking well and feeling nice. When I wear a nice suit that's how I feel. But most of the time I'm in jeans and a T-shirt. I don't know whether it comes naturally but I just like to feel comfortable more than anything – even when I was a young kid. When I was seven years old I was pageboy at a wedding. I had the choice of this one suit and another suit which was knickerbockers, a pair of long white socks and a pair of, like, ballet shoes and I chose that. So I don't know whether it comes naturally to me but I've always liked to look nice.' It was hardly surprising, in the circumstances, that he ended up wearing a sarong.

There was also some talk of the Beckham offspring pursuing a pop career. David had become friendly with the rapper Snoop Dogg, and the latter was keen that his sons, Corde, 15, and Cordell, 12, should link up with Brooklyn, who was now 11, Romeo, eight, and five-year-old Cruz to produce a song.

'Beckham's three boys have never known anything but the spotlight since they were born and if they have the talent of their mom and dad then they are destined for big things,' said Snoop. 'Corde and Cordell really want to get into the record industry and if they formed a group with the Beckham boys I think they could be really successful.

'I think probably only Brooklyn is old enough to be in the group yet but as soon as Romeo and Cruz are old enough they can join the mix, man. I have already talked with Bow Wow and Soulja Boy about adding vocals to their single and they are in. With me, David and Victoria behind them they would be unstoppable. I haven't put it to David yet. But when he is back in LA I will have a meeting organised. I don't want to rush things but I can't see why their first single should not be out by Christmas. What that boy can do with a ball is pretty tight. My boys loved it and I always said I wanted to repay the favour. David and I have talked about several projects in the past and a lot of things like movies and clothing ranges have been mentioned. But neither of us have had time to give to a project.'

Living in LA, it was almost inevitable that David would get caught up in LA-style preoccupations, and so it proved. There were reports that David had become an aficionado of Bikram yoga: 'David was introduced to Bikram by basketball legend Kareem Abdul-Jabbar at a steakhouse in Los Angeles a few years back,' said a source. 'Kareem told Beckham how regular Bikram yoga sessions would help heal his body, relax his mind and help him carry on playing football for years to come. At first David was sceptical it would really make a difference to his body but after a one-on-one session David instantly fell in love with the technique and has been doing it ever since. Victoria is a big fan and the pair of them often have a session together when they have time. Bikram yoga is becoming incredibly popular in LA and he's also been roping in his celebrity pals for workouts. David thinks Bikram yoga has really helped him get his fitness and focus back. He is determined to play top level football until he's past 40 and he is also adamant his international career is not over. At first he thought it was just another LA fad but after trying it out he's addicted. Not only does he feel stronger but the regime is also helping to keep him relaxed.'

So how long can he go on? David has certainly defied all expectations so far and he may well manage to carry on playing until he is over 40. But, especially given where he now lives, there are increasing suspicions that he is hoping to have a film career. David voice is now noticeably lower than it was when he was younger and he is certainly conscious of his appearance. He has often said that he is not interested in becoming a manager, so it is possible that he will look to entertainment when he does hang up his boots.

Whatever he does next, however, David Beckham has changed footballing history. On the one hand, he is one of the best players in the world; on the other, by cultivating the image that he has, he has shown that footballers do not need to be macho hardmen, but can be loving husbands and fathers with an interest in cooking and fashion. No other sportsman on the planet comes close to touching him in terms of profile or wealth; he has succeeded where other European players have failed, in joining an American club and yet still remaining in the top ranks of the game. His marriage endures; his children adore him. Family rifts have been mended and the future looks brighter than ever. There's only one David Beckham – and that doesn't look set to change anytime soon.